PRAISE FOR
SPIRIT CLANS

"Grounded in a deep belief that all of life is interconnected, David Carson invites the reader to explore the animal kingdom, identifying the spirit clans that can give strength and guidance. He writes with a quiet authority that casts a storyteller's spell. This book brings enchantment to the quest for self-knowledge. David Carson is truly a shaman."

—Julia Cameron, bestselling author of
The Artist's Way

"Spirit Clans is a powerfully told book of remembrance, returning ancient truths to the heart/mind of modern humanity through the magic of language and symbol. Above all else, it is a book of healing for a deeply wounded world that has temporarily forgotten its Earth and Sky roots and desperately needs to remember them. Read and remember, and by so doing heal yourself by rejoining with your sacred roots for now and evermore."

—Harlan Margold, author of The Alchemist's
Almanach, member of the Wolf Clan

SPIRIT CLANS

NATIVE WISDOM FOR
PERSONAL POWER AND GUIDANCE

SPIRIT CLANS

Native Wisdom for Personal Power and Guidance

DAVID CARSON

Foreword by Steven D. Farmer, phd

HAMPTON ROADS

Cover design by Jim Warner
Interior by Maureen Forys, Happenstance Type-O-Rama
Typeset in Neutraface Text and Lithos Pro

Hampton Roads Publishing Company, Inc.
Charlottesville, VA 22906
Distributed by Red Wheel/Weiser, LLC
www.redwheelweiser.com

Sign up for our newsletter and special offers by going to
www.redwheelweiser.com/newsletter.

ISBN: 978-1-57174-840-9
Library of Congress Cataloging-in-Publication Data available upon
request.

Printed in Canada
MAR

10 9 8 7 6 5 4 3 2 1

There is no death. Only a change of worlds.

Attributed to Chief Seattle.

In each life the human spirit appears as a repetition of itself with the fruits of its former experiences in previous lives.

—Rudolf Steiner

Memory and impression have similar forms. They give birth to our tendencies, which operate continuously to shape our lives, even if their cause is separated from their effect by time, by place, or by lifetimes.

Translated by Alistair Shearer from
The Yoga Sutras of Patanjali.

In memoriam to a beautiful being,
Fluffy, our cat, d. 2017.

CONTENTS

CONTENTS

ACKNOWLEDGMENTS

Collaboration is the nature of the creative process. I would like to thank my extraordinary daughters, Jacqui, Sara, Greta, Maggie, and Elizabeth for their invaluable comments and thoughts, and my dear friend Rhonda for her deep knowledge of all things spiritual and esoteric. Thank you to the people at Red Wheel/Weiser and Hampton Roads Publishing, especially senior acquisitions editor, Christine LeBlond, managing editor, Jane Hagaman, and copyeditor, Lauren Ayer. And finally, thank you to my partner, Karen—your encouragement and expertise never fail to inspire.

FOREWORD

Having just returned from an intense four-day retreat in the high desert of Joshua Tree, one of my favorite places on the Earth, I was delighted to be given the opportunity to review and write this foreword for *Spirit Clans—Native Wisdom for Personal Power and Guidance*. During the retreat, which focused on contemporary shamanic practices, participants received messages from the animals and plants inhabiting the land. The messages from Spirit conveyed through these "representatives" can be immensely helpful in guiding us along our spiritual path.

In *Spirit Clans*, David Carson, co-creator of the very popular *Medicine Cards* oracle deck, has taken this concept further, describing how each of us is profoundly related to a particular expression of Spirit, whether animal, plant, or other earth element. Not only that, but he also describes how our relationship with this aspect extends through many lifetimes, stretching back to our earliest ancestors who had developed an intimate affiliation with a specific plant, animal, or other naturally occurring life form. This is your Spirit Clan. The life form that is at the center is the thread that can provide greater understanding of your lineage and characteristics, and offer a detailed road map of your spiritual journey.

David describes several ways you can discover your Spirit Clan and thus "reconnect with the primal energy of your original Spirit Clan." This leads to a deepening of your spiritual practice and understanding of yourself. He offers a compendium of Spirit Clans from A to Z, each one detailing the attributes of being associated with this lineage as well as stories that speak to the soul of anyone who identifies with that particular clan.

Read this book slowly and try some of the methods that I'm sure will be helpful in identifying your clan. Meditate, journey, contemplate that connection once you discover it and you'll find a greater understanding and satisfaction with your purpose in this lifetime.

—DR. STEVEN FARMER, author of *Animal Spirit Guides and Sacred Ceremony*. For more information, go to *EarthMagic.net*.

1

HOH

TURTLE ISLAND

From the dark waters, she rose.

The thunder roared and the waves crashed.

The rains beat and the rain slashed winds whipped.

Still the Mother Turtle rose. She rose high. She rose fast, the great shell of her body stretching in every direction, north to south, distances beyond knowing. East to west. Still she rose.

Still she rose.

Her green head extended, bending back,

Two immense eyes spiking red above the dark turbulent sea, the boiling dark waters.

She pushed upward, the surf breaking on thousands and thousands of miles of dark ocean.

Coming up in froth and foam and water rolling away.

A deep green plated shell, the turtle—as though a large crust of the earth had broken free and pushed to the surface.

When she at last rested during eons of creation she was covered over and became land—an island—Turtle Island, our mother underfoot. Trees grew. Plants grew. Slowly, animals came, every kind of animal. They came.

And then the people, they came. Clans were born. And tribes and nations. And they made their camps upon every part of her, upon Turtle Island, upon her back. It was good, this sacred island we walk upon.

We are all related.

The North American continent has always been known as Turtle Island to Native Americans. All the land, all the forests, the mountains, lakes, and rivers are carried on the great turtle's back. All of the people, animals, fish, birds—all of life— we live on Turtle Island and all things are interconnected.

2

THE COMING OF
THE SPIRIT CLANS

Thunder spoke in the beginning of the world, launching the long process of evolution. The world was once dark and the people were huddled together, cold and hungry and praying for light. Suddenly, the world was split in two by lightning. There was a long, frightening growl. First Thunder was heard—so fearful and terrifying that it made the people scatter in every direction.

When small groups of these earliest humans met an animal or other entity such as a tree, a stone, a cloud, or some other magical being, they pleaded, "We are weak. Will you give us instructions and teach us so that we may live?" If the animal or other entity was willing to teach them, these humans became followers of that being and that being became their clan teacher and guide—the animated spirit of the clan. This, as is told in oral history and tribal myth, is how the original spirit clans were formed.

3

WHAT IS A
SPIRIT CLAN?

There is evidence that our early ancestors roamed the earth over eight hundred thousand years ago. Humans were not the dominant species—far from it. But humans did have a strong survival instinct. Spirit clans were born from the need of the human species to evolve. From the animals, humans learned how to feed and shelter themselves. Humans banded together in this new way and developed a social order. We owe our survival, our very existence, to the wisdom teachings of spiritual clans.

Spirit clans are not power animals. Power animals are personal spirit guides exclusive to an individual. Power animals emerge from visions, dreams, and meditations or other shamanic experiences. They can be mammals, birds, reptiles, or even mythical creatures such as unicorns, dragons, or winged horses or other winged animals. Power animals lend wisdom and add to personal power.

A clan, say, the Eagle Clan, could align with your power animal. Eagle could be your power animal and your clan lineage as well. A power animal facilitates personal power. A spirit clan is the original organized group with the imprint of our initial soul development, our spirit. We all have a spirit clan, a burning light in our heart that has been covered over. It was love as taught by these spirit clans that guided our evolution and survival. Your spirit clan was truly your original blessing and each of us carries its memories.

Many clans are guided by animal spirits, but a clan could just as easily be informed by a plant or even an object such as a rock or shell or an arrow or even an element such as fire. These clan totems and their teachings were at the mystic center of the clans. The clans were an identity, a sure source of nurture, protection, and a reservoir of powerful synergistic energy. Spirit clans were the first to teach us the meaning of being and provided guidance on how to live a good, meaningful, and transcendent life.

There were countless Spirit Clans over the globe and therefore your Spirit Clan does not have to be mentioned in this book. Clans represent our most ancient spiritual roots, our first coding, and first understanding at our mystical center. A spirit clan is considered to be your parent, your spirit mother and father. This knowledge can carry you over the dark waters of confusion. Finding your spirit clan can empower you, make you stronger, and awaken you. Knowing your clan will help you survive and thrive in these tumultuous, confusing, and shifting times.

Spiritual clans exist as spirit transcending countries and cultures, time and space. What we bind in spirit manifests. When we link with a kindred person from our spirit clan, a powerful synergy ensues. Where two or more people meet with the same spiritual objective, the energy increases a hundredfold. Spirit clans can unify us in this time of divisiveness. Their light will shine, inspiring a renewal and a warmth of spirit within our hearts.

Self-understanding is the key. Not knowing one's roots can result in true feelings of loss and separation. Everyone has an original clan. It is part of our heritage. Your clan came from ancient beginnings. Clans furnish an indescribable connection to the source of all life. A clan is the true Holy Grail, a spiritual search within ourselves.

Clan teachings and clan wisdom were kept by women. Clan chiefs, men and women, were selected by the Clan Mother, who was responsible for passing down all of the clan traditions. Everyone, knowingly or unknowingly, is born into an original spirit clan. Accordingly, individuals are forbidden to marry a member of their own clan because each member is considered to be a spiritual brother or sister.

Clans are spiritual in nature and do not exist as formal institutions. Rather, your clan is solely a spiritual bonding with your antediluvian self, your beginning, your orientation of being, and your most ancient identity. Spiritual clans burn in the heart and are a walkway to understanding who we are.

Clans predate recorded history. Clan memories are contained in intrapsychic phenomena hidden in our collective unconscious. Clans are transpersonal but also personal. Your clan is unique and specific to you as an individual.

With the exception of some tribal people and various aboriginal cultures, spirit clans exist in the margins, at various intersections of coincidence and fate. They are highly important to self-understanding and the information gleaned from this subjective discovery is infused with power, a reintroduction of the primal forces that have molded your life. We go backward in that quantity known as time to our first existential memories at the center of being.

Today, there are numerous women's and men's societies, fragments of leftover and forgotten spiritual clans. For instance, some of the women's societies greeted, honored, and cared for veterans returning from wars. Some keep genealogies and lineages. Some keep ancient power objects such as pipes and sacred medicine bundles. There are singing societies committed to preserving power songs and dance songs. Some of these societies were hatched from the disintegration of long-forgotten clans. The societies are keepers of ceremonial knowledge that would have been lost or destroyed. Because of these societies and because of clans and their connection to the ancient past, the sacredness continues.

This book is simply a remembering book, a possibility book—a hope that you will find an attraction to a great power within that you cannot resist or escape. I pray you find the hidden map to your spirit clan somewhere inside these pages, that you find your right path and familiar way, and that you will bring this remembering back into your life.

4

⚔️◀◀◀━━╢O╟━━▶▶▶

THE PATH OF
THE SHAMAN

Ancient shamans were the first psychologists. Shamans could read you. They could see you and what your issues and difficulties were. They knew your clan and knew what medicine or song or action to give you according to your clan.

They would sing you a song, perhaps a chant answering all your questions. The song could last for minutes or the entire day and into the night. Inside the song was a great vision, a great knowing. They did not talk. They sang. They drummed. They touched with a feather and woke up new places inside you.

When they divined you, it was communicated in song. The song enveloped you. They sang that all matter is sacred, starborn, be it plant, animal, or any child or creature of earth. The words held you in their heart. They sang that there are many phases, many lifetimes, within the fiery waters of spirit, within the vast expanse of your being. The song bathed you and wove in and around and through you and took away your suffering.

Shamans are healers—medicine people, aboriginal power doctors, and tribal practitioners. They divine, perform rituals, and have many unique skills including remote viewing and communicating with animals. They are intercessors between the natural world and supernatural realms. The word "shaman" comes from Siberia, where it meant a person of service. Now the word is no longer culture specific and is used far and wide to describe people who are believed to possess numinous power.

Shamans are connected to nature and to the spirit of animals. They know that every animal is a teacher. Those who have experienced shamanic training and have discovered their animal allies have learned that we have the ability to retrieve levels of understanding through close connection with animals. By undertaking inner explorations to revitalize these lost memories, we can renew vitality and increase our awareness. This way sings to the heart.

Animals possess attributes that are archetypes of deeper knowledge. Trees, rocks, lakes, and rivers also have much to impart and these natural creatures, objects, and phenomena contain deities and supernatural powers. Each of us is bonded with this knowledge on some level. This initial bonding held the nature and beginning of our ancestral spirit clans, our first social identities. Clan teachings, in one way or another, led us from the primeval ooze to today's technocracy.

Shamans have experienced many planes of existence, the everyday world, and many varieties of the supernatural.

They read the signs and know about unseen things. They are each unique to their culture complex, patterns, and traits. Some are dreamers, experts on dreams and dream interpretation. They are familiar with the supernatural world and in communication with good and evil spirits. Some are spellbinders. Some may be seers and prophets. They often have uncanny gifts such as the ability to locate lost or stolen items, find game, forecast the weather, and heal at a distance. Today, there are urban shamans who point out that not only do powerful spirits dwell in trees, lakes, mountains, and in all of nature, but also in our automobiles, computers, cell phones, garbage disposals, and other gadgets. Even buildings—old grandfather buildings or contemporary structures—have a spirit.

Shamans are power brokers and masters of spiritual energy. They can help you in many ways—remedying imbalance, conquering fear, finding your right path, finding your particular power places, and waking up lost and hidden aspects of your being. Once you are imbued with power, a shaman can lead you to your primary clanship and original blessings. This transfer of power can happen in seconds or over a long apprenticeship lasting years.

Shamans were the "chosen ones" who had access to the spirit world. They could communicate with a clan spirit, interpreting that spirit's wishes to instruct the clan. As an example, the snake teaches cunning, wisdom, and balance, and people in that clan exhibit those attributes. Snake Clan people know how to keep silent and, when necessary, strike with great force. Some tribal people maintain that snakes control the weather, and without placating the benevolent snake, spirit crops would die. Crops need rainfall to grow and it is the shaman who intercedes with the snake spirit to keep harmony in the natural world. Snakes and humans together participate in rainmaking ceremonies, which bring balance, healing, and equilibrium to the earth in a most elemental way. Shamans from snake clans are often called upon to perform these ceremonies.

Animals speak to us in unique ways and all shaman cultures know this. The shaman knows that animals and humans are connected with an unbreakable bond. What threatens insects, fish, mammals, reptiles, and birds will sooner or later befall humans. He is in a constant battle to adjust negative influences and restore a natural balance bringing us closer to nature. This, in turn, will benefit all of life and the planet itself.

Remember that spirit clans exist at the foundation of consciousness, a powerful centering place and the place to reclaim original powers. The doorway to your secret lost self, your clan, can open for you. It opens to the returning matrix inside the lodge of lost remembering that which is now hidden.

There are numerous ways to access this "remembering" via shamanic techniques such as dreams, visions, altered states, using past life regression, or one-on-one training with a shaman. These approaches can help you identify and find your particular and unique ancestral clan and claim it as your own.

DREAMS

Dreams are symbol laden, but the symbols are unique to the dreamer. One must ask themselves what these important objects, people, animals, places, and symbols are indicating. Obviously skills in dreaming take training and develop over time. The secret of dreams, of course, is to pay attention and listen. Consider dreams as a road sign, a map that must be followed.

Engaging in dream practices requires patience and dedication. It may necessitate a deconstruction of beliefs. One must first learn to interact within the dream when engaging with significant objects, plants, animals, or people, in order to ask for their help and guidance. These are the mentors and counselors on your quest. Carlos Castaneda referred to this technique as "lucid dreaming." In dreams, you may discover connections and clues leading you to your spirit clan.

Another method is to ask your dreams and your dream-body to seek out and put you in contact with your collective clan. This is facilitated by intent, deliberate dream programing. Shamans who teach dreaming often instruct a dream apprentice to consciously acquire the ability to use their hands in dreams. Next, learning to walk in dreams is taught. Once mastered, the dream apprentice can learn how to seek and find their original spirit clan. If you follow this path, you may find yourself in the midst of your spirit clan while dreaming. You will be able to interact and know your original clan, and this door will have opened for you.

Dreams can wake up past life memories. Many people have reported that they have heard drumming and singing in dreams. They have seen flickering campfires and silhouettes of shadowy people. Some people return to these dreams to discover a clan mother or clan chief. Dreams can bring you important connections to your ancestral past.

VISIONS

Visions are a powerful message leading to your spirit clan. Visions are personal—a form of heightened consciousness. There are records of visions dating back to the first vestiges of human civilizations. Visions transcend rational thought and occur somewhere inside a deep mystical state. Some visionaries say that their visions are pure ecstasy. Visions range from the spectacular to the mundane, from prophetic to troubling and puzzling. Sometimes people spend a lifetime unraveling the meaning of their visions.

Much holy writ contains visionary material. The Torah, the Bible, and the Koran recount many visionary episodes. There are the incredible visions of Hermes recounting a meeting with Osiris who instructs him on the path of souls. St. Teresa of Avila, St. Catherine of Siena, and St. John the Divine are all famous visionaries. All through history there are visionary accounts of angels, devils, goddesses, gods, and brilliant beings of light.

Visions often come to spiritually oriented individuals. There may be one vision or a series of them. Many visions, if not most, are religious or spiritual in nature. Visions may come during prayer or meditation, sitting in a church, or on a mountaintop. You could experience one during a stroll in a park or sitting at a table in a café. Like dreams, visions can also contain a past life experience.

ALTERED STATES

Most indigenous cultures with shamanic traditions have or had ways to foster altered states of consciousness. With training, some of these techniques can take us to the original cause within our early human evolution and to the source of our spirit clan. Some of these techniques are thousands of years old. There are many methods to bring about altered states. Some can be initiated by chanting, isolation, sleep deprivation, fasting, breath control, or dancing. Many psychotropic plants and drugs can also induce them—alcohol, tobacco, peyote, ayahuasca, LSD, DMT, psychedelic mushrooms, and many other substances may facilitate a deep inner connection with the numinous.

Partakers of these drugs are often able to leap out of the body or plunge into the deep earth, where they are able to visit and converse with ancestors. They may fly to the highest heaven and enter many other realms. They may be able to speak to power animals or personal guides or see what is going on in distant places in ordinary reality.

PAST LIFE REGRESSION

Past life regression is a hypnotic method to recover past life memories. After an ideal session, one will be able to recall and later record one's past life experience. One may sense, see, hear, or have an insight into their first dawn of awareness as a human organism.

Past life regression is spiritual work and provides access to your spirit clan. Accordingly, spiritual growth and purpose are highlighted in each soul's progression through a sequence of lifetimes.

During past life regression, you must trust yourself, have detachment, and be able to see and experience a past life with no emotion. You must go back to your first incarnation—that initial spark of self-awareness and awakened consciousness. A qualified hypnotist or therapist can use hypnosis or guided meditation to connect you to your first past life memories. The goal is to remember the spiritual gifts that were your first guide. You must ascertain where they are within this ancient memory. What is the landscape? Who have they bonded with? What is their clan and what are the teachings of the clan? You must hold these remembrances and bravely begin your journey through the multiple lifetimes and parallel selves you have experienced until the present time.

Past life regression often gives insights into obstructions—uncanny insights into the reasons for our repetitive detrimental actions. It can spotlight the causes of deep-seated anxieties and clear the negative energy around them. Our personal affairs become easier. We become less reactive because past life traumas are resolved and no longer hold sway. We find within ourselves new talents and lost abilities. These are just a few of the virtues of past life regression.

Past life regression is spiritual in nature and can lead to powerful realizations applicable to present life. In most cases, people who are unstable should not attempt past life regression without a qualified regressionist, a person who is versed in inner landscapes and time travel with its transformational potential.

A past life retrieval is a return to a lost memory that is lodged in our energetic interface with the universe, the world of creation and co-creation. Humans are yoked with the cosmos. We possess an electro-psycho-magnetic constitution, which is to say, a complicated network of cosmic wave receptors of the supra-knowing energy that is traveling through space.

Consciousness consists of three subjective parts: the unconscious, the conscious, and the supraconscious. Our unconscious can be a reservoir of suppressed content, all that is unpleasant in our lives that we have been unable to process, an iceberg of confusion and buried pain. The unconscious is tasked with keeping our heart beating, our lungs breathing, and other life systems going.

Our conscious mind, however, is our take on reality—what we believe to be happening and true. It is the awareness of the present moment, what may be going on outside ourselves. It defines our social norms. It is our thinking apparatus, the locus of our subjective mental functions.

The supraconscious mind is the mind outside our mind. It is the tapestry of universal understanding. It is the transcendent mind that knows the all and the everything. It is our most profound and insightful mind, a mind possessing true wisdom. The best way to process a past life memory is to stay in supraconsciousness while examining the conscious and the unconscious.

You can gain much benefit from past life regression and seeing your enduring habit patterns. You may realize the reason for ailments and attachments, and recognize buried suppressed gifts. And most importantly, you can access your original clan and the path you have followed through many lives.

Before participating in past life regression, try to abstain from media for a period of time. Do not concern yourself with the frenetic group mind. Try to merge with the simultaneousness of your spirit in other lifetimes by being open to all possibilities. Above all, let your heart and intuition guide you to memories long suppressed. Open yourself to creative remembering by allowing your mind to merge with the flow of universal consciousness. Your past lives and your clan will find you, if you will but agree to it.

TRAINING WITH A SHAMAN

There is no "how to" or easy road with shamanic training. You might begin by reading some of the great books on the subject of shamanism that have been written by such writers as Carlos Castaneda, Frank Waters, Black Elk, John Stands In Timber, and Tom Yellowtail. *Seven Arrows* by Hyemeyohsts Storm was one of the first books with a clear, understandable explanation of the medicine wheel, a major shamanic tool. *Rainforest Shamans: Essays on the Tukano Indians of the Northwest Amazon* and *Entering the Circle: Ancient Secrets of Siberian Wisdom Discovered by a Russian Psychiatrist*, a work by Dr. Olga Kharitidi, are excellent shamanic source material. The works of Hermann Hesse, the great German romantic metafictional novelist, are imbued with a clear Western mystical vision as contained within the complexity of modern life.

Studying anthropology and reading the classics of Joseph Campbell, Margaret Mead, Claude Lévi-Strauss, James George Frazer, and others can also help you on your journey of discovery.

Armed with some of the basics, you can experiment with accessing a powerful shamanic archetype. You might fashion a clay doll and create your own shaman. Imbue this representation with energy, prayer, smudging with sage smoke, and so on. Call in shaman spirits from the ethers. Let this being become a real presence in your imagination. Let your shaman be informed by the shaman inside yourself. We have boundless inner knowing. The act of creating a shaman can be your beginning apprenticeship. Meditate on your shaman. Do as you are asked by this wise teacher. This is an act of power. If you can create a perfect shaman in spirit, one will surely manifest in your life.

Authentic shamanic apprenticeship can be difficult. It can mean you will have to walk a long gauntlet of tests. Shamans are often pranksters who send you up twisted trails that lead nowhere. They laugh at you. They might destroy everything you possess—every important concept you have. A good shaman will pick your pockets and spend all your money. They might belittle your ethnicity and stomp your icons into the ground. And when you are completely lost and confused, they will take you by the hand and lead you to true power.

If you create your own shaman, a sort of mock shaman, beforehand, you may be able to forgo a lot of the mind-bending shocks of genuine apprenticeship. If it is your destiny, the shaman will come in actual human form.

5

THE SPIRIT CLANS
REVEALED

ALLIGATOR

It's always tempting, but resist the urge to wrestle with an alligator.

Protected by thick scales, the alligator has a long olive colored body with a powerful tail, strong limbs, webbed feet, and a rounded snout. No lower teeth are showing when its jaws are closed. When it strikes, it is with considerable bite force. The alligator is dangerous, ferocious. Destructive and creative, it plays its role in the harmonies and disharmonies of the world. It swims in the primordial waters of the mind.

Whatever else is going on, the enigmatic alligator, the largest reptile on the North American continent, eyes peeking just above the water line and the rest of its body submerged, watches. This creature has been on earth over two hundred million years, watching. Alligator lives in many simultaneous worlds.

Alligator Clan people are unseen, just as alligators stay hidden in muddy water. They watch and wait. They possess incredible psychic abilities. They are ancient souls who can access the Akashic records, a compendium of knowledge existing in the ethers recounting all human events, emotions, thoughts, words, deeds, and intentions that have ever occurred in the time and space continuum of human life. It is the Book of Being and exerts influence over everything we do. It is the Tablet of All Souls and bears witness to all our relations, descendants, and future lives. Alligator Clan people are said to be able to review these records at will. They are the avatars existing beyond our human understanding.

They have many mystical qualities and know the laws of the cosmos. They have a unique relationship with time, dimensionality, and the material world.

The moon, as it was once told by the native people who inhabited the bayou country, is an egg laid by the Alligator Mother when she slipped between worlds. The egg is still incubating there, but when it cracks open and the new alligator emerges, it will signal a new beginning, a new world—the next world to come.

Some elders say this has already happened—the egg has broken. The alligator has hatched and it swims through the dark night skies. This present world is done. It has cracked open and we have entered a new cyber frontier—an e-world that is just beginning but will lead to a perfect bliss and utopia.

Alligators are the mysterious and ancient ones. They exist in harmony with the creative and destructive principle. This clan brings inner and outer strength. Like eggs deposited in the warm sand on the river bank that are waiting to be hatched, the Alligator Clan brings a new birth and a new life.

Alligator Clan members are the most observant ones, the most patient ones. To find them, you must also become observant and patient. Look for powerful eyes that see and encompass many aspects of knowing, eyes that abide only with truth. When you can acknowledge them, they in turn will acknowledge you. And this is the understanding that admits you to this ancient clan.

ANT

Ants evolved from wasplike creatures long before human beings showed up. They may be small but they are also very strong and can lift a hundred times their weight. Ants are active and community minded. They create harmony and show you how to work effortlessly and without complaining. They make a plan and stick to it. They expend the least amount of energy but never avoid hard work.

Members of the Ant Clan have many powers such as industriousness, order, and perseverance. When dealing with ants in a disrespectful way, watch that you don't get stung. Certain Ant Clan people are said to be able to call two human-sized wizards from the entrance to an ant mound. These two beings are rather like genies who will grant you wishes and do your bidding. Therefore, you might want to sit and meditate near an ant mound to see what sort of medicine they might be willing to bestow on you.

There is a story of a poor woman who was picking berries when her village was attacked. Her children and relatives were murdered. She went crazy, wandering in the forest for days not eating, and sleeping on the cold, uncomfortable ground. As she was walking, she saw a tall woman in a reddish dress wearing a cape with a hood over her head. When she got close to her, she realized the woman was an apparition standing by a large ant mound.

"My poor child, my daughter, take this hickory stick and draw a deep circle around the edges of the ant mound. When this is done, speak into the entrance and ask the ants for anything you want." The hooded woman handed her the long stick and vanished before her eyes. The poor woman did as she was told. She spoke to the ants in the encircled ant mound and said, "I have lost everything important to me, but I beg you to make me want to live again."

She made her way back to her ruined village and found her old tipi. All her possessions had been stolen or destroyed—her soft buffalo robes, her clothing, and other things were gone. The lodge poles were shattered and broken. Nothing usable from her former life remained.

Once more, she was about to give way to utter despair, when four surviving women came to her. They pointed out the most beautiful tipi she had ever seen. "This is yours," the women told her excitedly. "A long line of people dressed in red and carrying many materials came here and built it for you. They worked tirelessly from dawn to dark for four days. They filled your tipi with all new possessions as well. You will want for nothing."

The woman could not believe her eyes. She had everything she might need and plenty more to share. She soon met a good young man and married him. They had several children and lived happily into old age. She was always grateful to the ant people and remembered where her good fortune had come from.

If you seek a way into this clan, pay attention to the workers, the ones who have been there and done that. Ask them for guidance. Let the industrious ant lead the way and perhaps you will find yourself working alongside like-minded people and accomplishing great wonders.

ANTELOPE

Antelope resemble deer, but instead of antlers, they have horns that are hollow at the base, resemble the shape of an ancient lyre, and don't shed. They are graceful and slender. They are elegant and have a certain lightness of being. They have discerning eyes. Their speed is proverbial.

Antelope have acute senses and quick reactions to danger. They are a litmus test against any menace and are rarely caught off guard or imperiled. Sensing a threat, they flee. They are swift and unlikely to ever be caught. They steal away from insensitive people or disharmonious crowds. However, when push comes to shove, they can be deadly fighters. They are lightning fast and will best most aggressors—whatever the battle, be it physical, intellectual, or even spiritual.

Members of the Antelope Clan are strong and have pronounced dichotomous personalities, but when they choose, they are aloof and indifferent. They can change their preferences as swiftly as they can run. They love nature, especially thick wooded forests where they feel protected, safe, and secure. They likewise love flat prairieland where they can open up and race to their heart's content.

Antelope Clan chiefs teach "the way of doing"—getting tasks done right now—as the only option. The antelope is a symbol for the crown of the head, which implies great intellectual abilities. They have fertile minds and often see opportunity where others don't. Antelope Clan people hate uncertainty and procrastination. If something is pressing, they do it. They don't stretch it out. Their motto is accomplishment, their message one of action and achievement.

It is the Antelope Clan that is responsible for creating the sipapu, the entrance to the lower world. Behind this open, earth-dug hole encircled with prayer sticks, there is an altar fashioned of leafy cottonwood branches. The altar holds bundles containing messenger spirits that will carry prayers to the inhabitants of the lower world, inhabitants such as ancestor spirits and all the master spirits of the animals.

The opening of the bundles is done by two Antelope Chiefs. The ceremony is performed in the spring and summer in the late evening. The unwrapping of the bundles is a solemn act. Power songs are sung as the messengers are released. The messenger spirits enter the sipapu and go deep into the earth to interact with creatures of the lower world. This honoring and acknowledgment keeps our earth pacified, free from fire, earthquakes, and other catastrophic events.

Like the deer, Antelope Clan people know what must be done by listening to their heart. They do what they say and walk their talk. They know. They do. They are able to get their point across and don't allow inefficient people to hold them back. Hook your wagon to an Antelope Clan person and you will have a great success. Carpe diem, antelope teaches. "Seize the day."

BADGER

Badgers have stout bodies and short, bushy tails. Their thick, powerful, slightly bowed legs make their ambling walk appear a bit clumsy. They sport long claws. Their fur is gray, black, and white with lighter colored underbodies. The badger's head is white with broad black stripes starting at the snout, covering the eyes and ears, and ending at the neck. Consider those stripes a warning.

Though the badger is not vicious by nature, favoring peace at all times, it is a most violent and terrible foe if provoked. Badger's claws are effective weapons and its teeth are long and sharp. When a badger closes its mouth, its jaws lock and hold without any effort on the animal's part. In other words, it will never let go.

Badger Clan people own their individuality and will defend it. They will also aggressively defend their clan. They are conservative and cautious but they meet problems with determined deeds. When badgers decide to act, they are quick to engage any aggressor.

Members of this clan are, generally speaking, prosperous because of their hard work and fortitude. That being said, they are obstinate and will never back down from a fight. It is just not in their nature. They scare many people away because they don't seem to know fear.

The Badger Clan stresses independent action. They know the earth so they are good agronomists. The Badger Clan chiefs light the new fires that are kept burning throughout the year and the fresh tribal fires are lit with old fire embers. Fame is no stranger to badgers and it comes to them without effort on their part, perhaps because they will always stand up for their principles.

Badger Clan people have good parenting skills, exhibiting love and tolerance toward their children. They resonate to the southern direction, the summertime of life, the place of children, the place of trust and innocence.

They are the guardians of the south and protectors of the little ones. They look out for all children, not just their own. They are noted healers and have extensive knowledge of medicinal roots and herbs. As a healer, the badger has no equal.

Perseverance is a quality of the Badger Clan. If you feel you have faced many challenges and undergone various levels of initiation and you continue to soldier on because you have been tested, it is probably time for you to kill your doubt and your darlings and become the great and heroic warrior you were meant to be. This is a sacred spiritual obligation before being admitted into the Badger Clan.

BEAR

Most bears are king-sized and intelligent. Most are omnivorous and eat meat, fish, plants, and insects, and are good at foraging, though pandas eat only bamboo. Black and brown bears are formidable, shaggy, and have strong legs and a long snout. They are highly active. Bears like to swim, climb trees, and scramble over mountainous terrain. They hibernate in winter.

Bears are armed with sharp, retractable claws. They are lightning fast at catching fish, especially salmon. They have great force and can ward off the most vicious of attacks. Bears are conspicuous creatures and you are not likely to miss them if they are anywhere near. They are quick to raid a beehive and will risk getting stung for the honey. They have been known to break into houses and rob pantries.

Most, but not all, bears are frightened of humans and shy away from them, but they can be aggressive and are best avoided. The grizzly bear is fearless and will attack a person even if they are mounted on a horse. Only the bravest of hunters would dare to face a grizzly bear in one-on-one combat. In such battles it was a toss-up as to who might win. Often as not it was the grizzly. If the hunter triumphed, he became a legendary figure whose fame spread far and wide.

Bear Clan people have strength, integrity, and power. Bears are the guardians of the west on the medicine wheel—the direction that symbolizes the autumn, darkness, and introspection. West is the "looks-within" place. Bears hibernate and know the inner territories, including dreams and visionary states.

Bears have many powers. They have warrior power and the fighting bear has strength and the clout to slay demons, outward and within. They are close to the spirit world, often communing with it while going about their regular business. There are medicine bears with their powers to heal, the shamans and mystic doctoring bears who know the medicine roots and herbs. There are tracking bears with the knowledge to see the signs in nature. With tracking comes wisdom and the power to predict the behavior of others. Bears track to the crossroads of differing possibilities. Bears track into self-awareness. Lastly, there are the mama bears. They are the ultimate providers, protectors, and guides, and raise their cubs with lovingkindness.

To find the Bear Clan, look to Ursa Minor, the Great Bear in the night sky, and at the tail end of that constellation, you will find the North Star to give direction. Your soul and your dreams will surely orient you. When you find your bearings, turn left, go west and you will discover the Bear Clan—within and without. You will become an expert in bear's teachings, expand yourself to become a Jack or a Jill of all spiritual trades. People in the Bear Clan are dreamers and visionaries. Dreams and visions are the best way to access this powerful clan.

BEAVER

Beavers are aquatic animals with brown fur, webbed hind feet, and flat, hairless tails that propel them wonderfully well through the water. They live in communities and make their lodges by clear creeks and rivers, wide springs and lakes. If the water isn't deep enough to suit them, they engineer dams in order to raise the level. They mostly work in the dark of night. Like humans, they have the ability to shape their environment to their liking.

Beaver Clan people are noted for their cutting and building. Beaver people know the water. They know a rewarding way of living. They are creative and nobody's fool. The Beaver Chief taught the clan to work hard and do their individual parts. They are social creatures. They are great healers and hold potent medicine dances. They are wise. They know the seasons. Their lodges are neat, trim, and tidy. Like Native America and the buffalo, beavers have nearly gone extinct. It's been touch and go. So far, Beaver's mysterious medicines always bring them back from the brink of destruction stronger than ever.

Go to the Beaver Clan people if you want to get things accomplished. They always have a project. They have control and focus when they work. They know designs and architecture. They are the hands-on builders of our civilization. If you have these qualities, you will be welcomed into this clan.

Go to the sage, old holy Beaver Woman to learn prayers, power songs, and curing rituals. The Beaver Clan way is the way of the pipe. They know secret plants and medicine roots and how to prepare and use them. They know how to use different ritual methods on themselves and on their lodge brothers and sisters to ward off evil.

The Beaver Clan embodies wise acts, idealism, and a true understanding of what is possible. Beavers build the healing lodges—lodges that not only exemplify great skill and craftsmanship but also are places of quiet surrender. Beaver Clan people know the simplest architectural forms where one can meet with the eternal. They are the people of community. Their lives are exemplary, always working unselfishly for the greater good, the highest order. Their work has a ripple effect that benefits all of humanity.

BLUEBIRD

Bluebirds are members of the thrush family. They came from the west long ago and their feathers are used in ceremony to guard that direction. The male has a blue head and wings. They appear blue to the eyes but they are not actually blue. The blue color is a trick of the light. Bluebird sings a happy, unique song and reminds us to do the same. Their songs are said to drive away mean and vengeful spirits. Bluebirds are gentle and timid yet they are spiritual messenger birds. They tell you to be aware of the splendor of the gift of life.

Bluebirds were once ugly, and received their blue color from bathing in a magical blue lake four times each morning. Bluebirds carry twisted medicine, the power to enchant and lift one to the Great Light. Some elders say that the Bluebird Clan has connections to unearthly visitors, unknown species, perhaps even beings from invisible or distant worlds.

The Bluebird Clan is associated with the weather and they predict it by their behavior, disappearing during inclement weather and appearing when the sun shines brightly. Some say bluebirds can even regulate the weather. Some say that bluebirds have ally, meaning friendly, winds.

Bluebirds are also associated with fertility and their feathers are given to women and kept for this purpose. Bluebird has come to symbolize happiness, but it is much more than simple happiness—it is inner acceptance, self-love, and peace. The bluebird way is a blissful way because of their spiritual communion with the upper world. Bluebird Clan people do not travel far from their clan. They don't mind living in tall apartment buildings or on mountaintops. They spread good cheer wherever they go.

Bluebirds were once common but no more. Count your blessings if you are able to see one, for it may be telling you that the sky is blue and the way is clear to pursue your dreams. The Bluebird Clan tells you to enjoy, to savor, and to share your good fortune and happiness with others. Their spiritual teaching is simple: always have a cheery attitude and this energy will transform you and others.

When the earth is green-growing, greet the sun with a bluebird song. Put away doubt. Let your heart be full of glee. Be happy because the evening sun will come soon enough. Open your eyes to the greatest happiness. Open your heart and blissfully follow the bluebird road to your clan.

BUFFALO

Buffalo have great value to Native America. They were found solely in North America and parts of Mexico. They prefer to live in vast herds. In the past they supplied most every necessity of life.

Buffalo are huge and hefty and are startling in appearance. They are so loaded down with a mass of hair, they are often called Old Woolies. Most all buffalo, numbering in the millions, were killed in a great slaughter during the 1800s. They once grazed the prairie lands and migrated all across Turtle Island. They are able to run at a fast clip when necessary. They often seem to bow beneath their own weight. Although buffalo were once on the brink of extinction, they endure. Buffalo populations are growing steadily. The buffalo is coming back.

Buffalo love to wallow in the mud and practically any mud hole will do but they will create their own when one is not readily available. All the buffalo needs is a little wet spot of earth. He throws himself down and twists around and about producing a circular, shallow pit that fills in with water and mud. He joyfully coats his entire body with a thick layer. The coating protects him from stinging insects and any number of gnats and flies.

The buffalo is holy. It meets our every requirement—physical and spiritual nourishment, shelter, and clothing. Buffalo are a symbol for prayer and abundant living. Buffalo forge ahead. They have strength and willpower. To be near a buffalo on the open plains is an awesome experience.

Buffalo Clan people are the great providers, loving and caring. The way of the buffalo is a way of high-mindedness and altruism, love and courage. The buffalo way embodies the spirit of giving, gratitude, and endless generosity. They are keepers of the knowledge of the invisible vibrations of prayer.

Members of this clan are understanding and sympathetic to the plight of unfortunate people. The needs of others are important to them—much more important than their own needs or desires. They are a welcome presence in this age of materialism and selfishness. They have been known to give away all their possessions to help those in need.

During Buffalo Clan meetings there are always prayers and a passing of the holy pipe. All relations are honored. The clan teaches respect and appreciation for the gifts we are given and a willingness to meet the spiritual and physical needs of others. To be in the Buffalo Clan, you must walk the road of humility, surrender, and spiritual power.

The Buffalo Clan is balm for anyone wishing to live a strong and peaceful life. The buffalo, giving its entire being and spirit to the people, shows us our dependence on one another. The Buffalo Clan is found by divine discernment. One travels the Buffalo path with an open heart and a love for all creation.

BUTTERFLY

Butterflies are free to fly, but first, they must crawl. The caterpillar constantly eats, hungry for life. It molts over and over, sloughing off its old skin. It grows large and turns into a chrysalis, where it appears to rest, but it is in fact hard at work, imagining and creating itself. Suddenly, a beautiful winged creature emerges, free to dance upon the winds.

The way of the butterfly is to flit joyfully from flower to flower on a quest for beauty, and the butterfly is said to teach the harmony of the soul's migration. Quiet transformation is their specialty. They can give clarity to your mental processes. They can assist you in finding the next step in your personal life or career. The Butterfly Clan keeps the migration legends and stories of the people.

Beautiful butterfly with her astonishing colors—go ahead and chase one if you are so inclined. There's no telling where it may lead. Some say if you follow one diligently, it will lead you to a great happiness and this is true in many stories. A young brave had a dream in which a departed aunt told him to go to a certain blooming flower-filled meadow and follow the first butterfly he encountered.

As the dream instructed, he followed the flitting butterfly a long distance for many hours until it landed on a nearby lovely flower. He cupped his hands, walking slowly toward the scissoring wings to fall upon and capture her. Before he could, the butterfly turned into a woman whose beauty was staggering. It was more than a friendship from the start and difficult to know who had captured whom.

The woman never lost her beauty and he was always the handsomest of the handsome. Of course they lived happily ever after. So it is said.

Butterflies travel a wide compass. Their element is air, the mind, mental. Their very dance around the tree of life is their gift. Monarch butterflies, to escape cold weather, migrate south. They congregate by thousands on certain trees, known as butterfly trees, along the way. Perhaps you, knowingly or unknowingly, are on a migratory road and looking for sanctuary. It is a long and oftentimes difficult but necessary journey that ends in full-blown magnificence.

Butterflies are great warriors related to the sun and to sunlight—flitting and darting—impossible to second guess. They ask about your imminent transformation. They are mystical beings that can transform your life through bold, new realizations. Who are you becoming with the passing of life's seasons?

The Butterfly Clan instructs you to go ahead and change. It teaches the cyclic nature of life and how to successfully negotiate change and find contentment with the turnings of the wheel of life. The Butterfly Clan is driven by an inner light and courage.

Butterfly people are always evolving, seeking change, and changing in their effortless effort. Let their energy and spirit surround you. You will find yourself having a color-filled, beautiful life.

CLOUD

There is no clear definition for the word *cloud*. The dictionary defines cloud as a vapor, as smoke, dust, a muddle, a visible mass, murkiness, swarm, multitude, a particle collection, and so on. The name cloud is a cloud-over of many definitions. It can be a cloud of insects, a cloud of birds. Today, we are even storing our clouds in a computer.

Clouds are positioned between earth and the upper world. Storm clouds bring rain and therefore fertility and growth. In this sense clouds are a benefit to all of humanity. Clouds connect us with spirit. Clouds are sky, not separate, forming and reforming. They are earth's ancient movie screen revealing the shape of things passed and things to come.

The red clouds, the blue and gray clouds, the clouds high above or laying low on the horizon, clouds of every ilk and shape, shadowed and white clouds, moving clouds, glowing clouds, dream clouds, shapeshifting clouds, merging clouds, transfiguring clouds, thunderheads—all are continuously moving, shifting.

Cloud Clan people are in a state of constant change as well. They live in the moment. They teach us of the impermanence of all things, of the illusion. They are connected with the afterlife and the cloud people above. They are often associated with the rain and rain cycles, and a copacetic relationship with animals. Members of the Cloud Clan often have haunting beauty, especially Cloud Clan women—obscure, dark, transcendental.

A woman married a cloud, they say. She climbed the sky and rested on a puffy, comfortable cloud and fell asleep.

A man, part cloud and part human, offered to marry her. She accepted and they lived in heavenly splendor for four years—until one day she told her husband that she had to return to her people. Before she left him to climb down to earth, he taught her how to sculpt clouds and make little animals and other living beings and bring them into form. He taught her that she could easily manifest her dreams.

Watch clouds but let them go their way. To chase a cloud is to chase a mirage. Disappearing, fluctuating in Rorschach randomness. Meaningful cloud images are sometimes seen by people living in the mist where things get clouded—faded petroglyphs of a mind gone camera obscura, gone dark and daunting.

Being a Cloud Clan person means staying observant and having a clear mind. You may experience uncertainty. You may suffer over some unrealistic belief. Let your mind meander. Follow the billowing buttermilk clouds. We ourselves are like clouds and shadows transforming—changing, always changing, impossible to grasp. Clouds are the teachings of the mystics—the dissolving of egos giving way to timelessness. Cloud Clan people, the same.

CORN

Corn is a domestic plant and must be cultivated. Growing corn, we are repaid a thousand times over. Hominy, succotash, cornmeal mush, and pone are examples of the hundreds of dishes that use corn as a main ingredient. Corn provides medicine and brings good health. The last ear of corn harvested holds a potent corn spirit. In certain pueblo cultures this ear is fashioned into a stylized doll and hung in the kitchen or elsewhere in the home. It sees to the bounty of the family, making sure everyone is well fed and happy.

Corn, known originally as maize, is an ancient and traditional crop. Corn was born from the Sun Father and the Lightning Mother. Corn symbolizes fertility, abundance, and life and is held sacred. Corn is nourishment. It sustains us. It feeds the people and has many spiritual lessons to teach.

Every part of the corn is used. Corn silk is made into a medicine tea, which is rich in antioxidants. Cornhusks are used to make various kinds of corn tamales. Corn pollen teaches about the earth goddess, the gift of life, peace, longevity, regeneration, and plenty. Corn pollen and corn meal are used in various ways in many sacred ceremonies. Corn pollen is considered sacred and offers access to a blessed place, a place of plenty.

Like kernels on an ear of corn, Corn Clan people are close to each other. They are united in their support for one another. They know how to work together as a group or how to work individually and separately. They work to maintain order and for the survival of the clan. Corn is sustenance but it is also a metaphor for how to live well.

Long ago Coyote danced and the corn grew. The first two humans, male and female, were born from two ears of corn. The male was born from white corn and the woman was born from yellow corn. Soon after, many people came. They became corn and they became people. The ones who planted themselves became corn. When coyote danced near the sown seed corn, the planted corn, it grew. And it continued to grow and feed the people forever afterward.

Corn pollen from the corn tassels symbolizes life and prayer. The pollen path is the beauty path. Pollen is used for blessing and in countless ceremonies. A pinch of corn pollen in the mouth reminds us that we are living prayers.

Corn Clan people exist in and understand community. Therefore, one needs to join into the spirit of community. Community is only as strong as the merits of its individual people. People who exhibit gratitude and traditional agrarian values are easily welcomed into the Corn Clan. They know we must work together and nourish one another.

COTTONWOOD

The cottonwood is a fast-growing, water-loving tree with white to gray bark and lustrous silver-green foliage.

Cottonwood is medicine. The inner bark is high in vitamin C and is used to treat this deficiency. Poultices made from the bark are used to reduce swelling and inflammation and for wound treatment.

The cottonwood tree transcends human ignorance and shows us the transitory nature of life as we know it. Trees are sacred. They talk to one another. Like all trees, cottonwoods connect three worlds, with roots in the lower world, the trunk grounded in earth, and its leaves in the air or upper world. The cottonwood has astounding life force and is used in many ceremonies. Unless used for ceremony and celebration, cutting down a cottonwood tree causes havoc in the spirit world. Tribal elders weep when it is needlessly felled. It is a magic tree when treated respectfully and with reverence. As the leaves rustle, and if one listens intently, answers to perplexing questions come. The great tree is a medium through which prayers are answered and solutions to difficulties become apparent. The tree furnishes a home for many animals and birds. A pantheon of spirit dolls, kachinas, are carved from cottonwood roots. Cottonwood is used in drum making and these drums are powerful tools used to bridge between worlds. Cottonwood is used to produce various other musical instruments such as whistles. It is used for prayer sticks. It is even used to make canoes.

Huge cottonwoods furnish shade and comfort inside the sheltering umbrella of its rippling heart-shaped leaves, a reminder of love and sacredness. When a cottonwood pole is used in ceremony, it is believed to be a direct link to the mysterious spiritual forces that govern creation. They are often used as tipi poles.

Members of the Cottonwood Clan are self-reliant. They are strong for one another with bright and loving dispositions. They are centered and always loyal, always elegant, always striving to reach spiritual heights. Cottonwood people are said to be star people, people with knowledge of distant worlds. Some in the Cottonwood Clan profess to have memories of Pleiadian life. They believe that very soon star people will return to the earth to keep us from total ruin, if they haven't already.

Cottonwood is the tree of life, a holy tree with a sacred center bringing visions and spiritual understanding. One tree is connected to all trees. Sit with your back pressed to the trunk of a cottonwood tree and feel the strength of its trunk, the comfort of its shade, its unconditional peace and acceptance.

COYOTE

Coyotes can be motley, bedraggled, and comical. They are much smaller than a wolf and have a coat with curious color combinations. They can be seen in Alaska down the west coast to Mexico and their territory includes much of the United States—even in big cities like Los Angeles. Coyotes are survivors.

Coyotes are said to be the great, unscrupulous tricksters famous in legend and song. The coyote's antics keep things moving. They are the necessary teacher without which life would be drab. They force change. They bring out the shadow self, and with it, all that is repressed. As has been said by various sages, you don't become enlightened by being sanctimonious and continually striving for goodness and light. You become enlightened by seeking within yourself, by finding the light hidden in your own darkness—your personal shadow.

One has only to listen in the dead of night to a howling coyote pack to sense their enormous presence. Coyotes are the first singers, the inventors of music. In that howl is a heartrending sadness, their songs expressing so many conflicting emotions—excitement, wonder, distress, sensitivity, and many other sentiments.

Members of the Coyote Clan, like their namesakes, may seem outrageous, vulgar ne'er-do-wells. They might be at the top of the heap—millionaires, billionaires, CEOs of multinational corporations, even the president of a country, or they might be the lowest of the low. One thing is certain, they are always good for a painful laugh.

In this complicated clan, coyote people are brilliant when working together—they are smart, cunning, and adaptable.

There's an old expression, however: "When thieves fall out as they inevitably do, there is hell to pay." More often than not, they are victims of their own machinations.

Coyotes are a massive bundle of contradictions. So are the people in the Coyote Clan. In myth coyotes are gods working tirelessly to create disharmony and disorder—in short, screwing things up. They are the magnificent pranksters—the coyote's motto is to do something rash now—now being the operative word. Because they adapt to every situation, in a sense every situation is new and offers a new opportunity to hustle someone.

As a last bit of coyote lore, they say that when you hear the yodel of a coyote outside your open bedroom window, soon afterward, your prayer will be answered. The question is, which prayer? The answered prayer will be long out of date or maybe for something you no longer want. For instance, you may have prayed to get out of jail. But first you may have to go back to jail to get out again. Better hope your coyote prayers were not selfish and that you were praying for the good of all.

Believe it or not, coyotes are holy. True, they make it hot for you, but they shove you through paralysis. They can help you process your worst hang-ups and get through them. Coyotes love to gamble. They play the long shots but most often they lose everything they own. You can play the odds too and gamble on coyote. When the icy winds blow and you hear the call of a coyote, follow it only if you must. Make sure you hide your money in your shoe and protect your wallet. The Coyote Clan is waiting to embrace you and teach you a few tricks.

CRANE

Cranes are slender, long-legged birds, usually found at the water's edge. Some are white and some are a light green, akin to olive with a trace of brown. The darker colored cranes' head and neck are a dark ash color. Adult cranes measure about four feet in length.

Cranes are beautiful creatures. They flow with a harmony of movement when they spread their wings and lift off and take to the sky. They are a symbol of spring and fidelity.

The flight of the crane is toward discovery. In working with crane energy, one can influence the fabric of reality. Cranes have fluidity. They are a symbol for long life and happy relationships—and most especially parental relationships between father and son. Cranes also symbolize hope. They offer you an opportunity to investigate your identity by taking a deep look at the workings of your life and then carefully examining what isn't working to make repairs. Cranes have self-knowledge and know exactly when and how to act. They are the perfect actualization of nothing more and nothing less to do—a teaching of how to expend the least amount of effort while reaping the greatest of rewards.

Members of the Crane Clan are graceful, balanced, and always exhibit strength and a polished smoothness. They are centered and poised. They are water people and have memories of being in the womb. Accordingly, they received spiritual teachings while being in a fetal state. These lessons are instilled in their very DNA. They have innate leadership gifts and enjoy long, fertile relationships.

Crane people have flexibility—rather than worrying about what isn't, they work with what is and change it for the better. They understand that the frantic hustle and bustle of the crowd leads nowhere. Instead, they teach the balance point. The Crane Clan teaches one to do less and less until they find the center of the whirlwind, launching a counterforce to the turbulence of our times.

Each day, cosmically speaking, you are standing in a place you have never been in a world just being born—a world that never existed until now. There are countless worlds before you and crane knows the best one to choose. Cranes know they can never go back to what was and that each moment holds infinity.

Find your deepest inner peace and you will make the quantum leap that propels you into the Crane Clan. You must get out of your own way and escape your current trajectory, your bondage and baggage. Hop out of this dense dimension that is holding you down with its leaden gravity, with its ignorance and false values. This clan will help you suppress your rational mind in order to realize that the universe is a big place and you—little you—are a part of the fabric of the universe. In that way you can be born anew into the kingdom of a new song, a new dance, a new spirituality—enfolded in the beautiful wings of the divinely beautiful crane and the welcoming, loving Crane Clan.

CRAWDAD

Crawdads are crustaceans. They have strong exoskeletons with a segmented tail and various appendages including pincers. They have ten legs attached to the abdomen area, legs that would bend at the knees, if they had knees. They don't. They motivate and shoot through the water like a fast-propelled underwater shark or a high-performance speedboat.

The crawdad lives in two simultaneous realities according to the Jena Band shaman in the southeast. The crawdad's big lesson is to let go, quit clutching, and release to spirit. The Jena are a complicated band who speak French. They are masters of the blowgun. They are defining a new tribal identity. Like the crawdad regenerates its limbs, so can people regenerate themselves if they pay attention to crawdad's teachings. Crawdads teach the plurality of worlds and how each world can enhance the other. There is a crossover. Crawdads are from the mud, the water, and the spiritual sky.

Crawdad Clan people are resolute. They are close to the water spirits. They are in touch with the underwater chiefs who teach how to bless and curse with water and have strange gifts brought from the water world. They know how to use water to their advantage. They have various mysterious powers. In ceremonies, a crawdad claw is used by a power doctor to scratch the hand to give it a strong grip. The crawdad scratch is also said to give great dexterity and special coordination between the thumb and fingers. The clan teaches tribal and personal responsibilities to one another by example. They are there when you need them most. Never underestimate crawdad's power to flow into your soul and help you during any difficult time.

Go to this clan for water fasts and rejuvenation, regeneration, and protection from enemies. They will show you how to move forward through obstacles and how to enlarge constructive environments you have created. They will help you shed outdated and limiting beliefs. They teach mobility, coping with rapid changes, and how to overcome fear. Because of their water connection, they can guide one to emotional maturity.

If you find yourself in a dance with the moon, seeing it regularly on the surface of water, and if you have dreams of past underwater lives, the Crawdad Clan may well be calling out to you, trying their best in the hidden dimensions to bring you into their fold. So listen, listen . . . in the dark of the night, transcend the mind and listen and see if your lost water sisters and brothers are calling for you to join them in the spiritual depths.

CROW

The crow is recognized by its beak and its wings and its harsh-sounding "caw." The birds are blue-black like the raven. In fact, crows resemble the raven in miniature. They have long memories and understand abstract concepts. They are highly observant and have excellent sight. Crows are hunting birds, but because of their size they are limited in what they can attack. They are omnivorous and there are few things they will not eat. They will steal the eggs of other birds. They love corn and are a menace to cornfields. They will eat lizards and small snakes. They eat worms, grubs, and all manner of insects. They are also scavengers and especially like dead animals.

Crows are the forceful seers and know what must be done. Their communication is strong. The direction of their caw's sound is as important as the exact intonation and pitch. Needless to say, when you feel threatened in this world, ask for their blessing and help. Leave them an offering, a cookie or some other treat. Crows have courage and many hidden, helping, and supernatural powers.

Crow Clan people know spiritual laws and bring forth cosmic communications that are falling down to earth. They are the transformers—the changers. A confrontation with the crow is always a confrontation with new possibilities. Crows came from the void before time existed. They play with light and darkness. They know the unknowable mysteries of creation and their clan keeps the knowledge of the most sacred laws.

Members of the Crow Clan have accepted their personal shadows. They know what is hidden and suppressed.

They do not fear darkness. From the darkness light is born and spirit is renewed. They cross thresholds and go past judgments and assumptions. These people can stretch or compress the elasticity of time, bending our consciousness. They teach that law is the shining path that cuts us through the void. They teach how to make the spirit flesh. They teach that spiritual law is forever and earthly law is, at most, brief.

Crows are the guardians of ethics and know that right and wrong are relative to one another. Crows have rules. Crows are the shapeshifters who understand their mission. In ceremony they honor their ancestors. If you are drawn to this clan, this murder of crows, and you fit the sophisticated crow mold of integrity and dignified honor, do not hesitate to pledge yourself to this august body.

DEER

Deer are plant-eating mammals found on every continent but Australia. There are many types of deer ranging in size and description. They prefer woodlands but adapt well to most habitats. Their color varies between red and brown and can turn grayish in the winter. Male deer have antlers.

The deer is a feminine symbol because of its gentleness and heart energy. Deer have lovely features. Their eyes are lustrous and their gaze is said to have an innocent purity—the very essence of compassion and benevolence. Deer just are. They never force or push their will, yet they are a potent energetic power. They are the power of the heart, a patient and tender empathy from which deer look upon the world with transcendent understanding and lovingkindness.

Deer Clan people are sensitive, loving, and inclusive. They are kind and supportive. They are the sweet medicine ones who see into pressing problems and have a specific message that will help you find the answer you need. At the very least they will lessen your anxiety and prevent a panic attack. Deer's teachings are of compassion, affection, and calmness. They are the devoted, true, and insightful ones. They do not tarry. Their sleekness and speed are proverbial and they are swift to act on your behalf.

Deer have superb awareness and keen senses. They are linked to peyote, and as such, are keepers of visionary states. Deer are open to the world and worlds beyond. Because of their antlers—their antenna, deer are thought to have developed a connection with a greater intelligence and to carry messages from other realms of possibility and awareness. Deer teach healing, midwifery, regeneration, and renewal. They are an energy of higher order and many people believe deer are their ancestral spirits.

Deer are very sacred in Native America. Deer shamans were the first curing shamans, the first to heal disease. Traditional deer dances are held in many places on Turtle Island. These fervent dances are usually tribe specific. There are many beautiful deer songs sung during these events. Usually these dances are held at night around a fire in a large ceremonial dance circle but there are many other times and places deer dances may be held.

If you feel you are stuck, find a deer track and follow it. You need to learn to walk through the imaginary wall that you have constructed in your mind, the brick wall that separates you from self-actualization. The deer offers you a doorway though this wall, a doorway that leads from illusion to liberation.

It is an axiom that if you follow your heart, it will lead you to the Deer Clan. If you find your way to the magical deer lodge and you enter, you will be welcomed with simple acceptance and love. To know love is to know peace. Peace will be with you ever more once you have taken the magical step into the spirit teachings of the deer.

DOG

Dogs are found all over the world. They have been long domesticated and are kept as pets. Dogs come in every shape and size between small and gigantic, in nearly every color and hue, and in a variety of characters and temperments. Males of the same breed are larger than females, generally speaking. Regardless, all dogs have power.

Once a man found a mysterious tipi. He entered and inside was every kind of dog, but they were not dogs at all. They were dog spirits, ghost dogs. They told the man to learn the secret language of dogs and teach it to other humans. The dogs told of their devotion to some humans. All agreed that dogs are the best companions.

Dog Clan people are guardians and protectors. The Dog Clan is a great clan comprising many subclans. One senses the spirit of canines around members of this clan. If you are stuck, ask them to sniff out the way forward or to protect your time and effort. They will help you find what you are looking for if you will but ask them. It is said that dogs can speak for you in the spirit world and be an intermediary acting on your behalf with ancestor spirits.

Most members of the Dog Clan are happiest and hardiest when they are in service. They have many friends who view them as steadfast and trustworthy, which of course, dogs are. When they sense trouble, they head into the center of the fray, and then, with their ferocious hackles up, they will have a go at any enemy or enemies you might have. They attack fervently and usually prevail.

When one thinks of dogged persistence and exactitude, dog power is there. Dog has the power to lead you unerringly on your path. The dog insists that you continue wagging your tail (be happy) and stay faithful to your vision. With the dog as your clan advisor, your expressive powers will never waver.

Naturally enough, there are many breeds within the Dog Clan—each with its own distinct characteristics and temperament. Many have specialized abilities. For instance, you may want to call on the spirit of the Greyhound when you want to speed your life along in pursuit of an important objective. Put the smell of victory in front of you and set loose the Greyhound spirit to propel you to success.

The tenacious Bulldog will take a big bite out of your troubles and won't let go until you are free of impediments. If you are lost, imagine the nose of a Pointer pointing the way homeward.

Dog Clan people have many virtues, the most recognizable being virtue itself. Dogs give without reserve. Each dog has his or her own merits. They can be shy, bold, or aggressive. They are all different. You can call on various dogs for help in almost any situation. Dog Clan members are loyal and will have no reluctance in giving support or facing danger. They all give unconditional love.

DUCK

Ducks are waterfowl from the same family as geese and swans. They are waterproof and can be found in fresh or sea water. They are versatile in selecting their living environment and are happy just about anywhere there is fresh water. Ducks love the marsh, lakes, rivers, ponds, and other watery places.

Wild ducks symbolize life force and they are at home in the water and the sky. They are migratory. They are harbingers of good news. Ducks, especially their eggs, symbolize sensitivity and mercy and also fidelity. Duck feathers symbolize fertility and happy marriages and are used in water ceremonies. Ducks are loyal guardians of pregnant women. They are nurturing to their young.

Members of the Duck Clan are masters of many dimensions. On land, sea, or sky, they are in their element. They can walk, fly, or swim, and even dive deep and spend long periods of time underwater. Duck Clan people will fake people out to lead them away from things they cherish and want to protect. They are happy and community minded. They are attractive and dress well. They like to fit in—fly in formation. They are very clear in what they want. They are resourceful and quick to seize opportunities. They can easily help others deal with emotional situations. Clan members never poison themselves with hatreds or the hatching of evil plans. They move on and let bygones be bygones. And they don't get confused. They dive into their unconscious to find the correct answer to their questions.

Duck dances are not unusual in Native America. Some of them feature the duck walk, a sort of duck mimic with waddling steps. However, there are many types of duck dances performed by various tribes, which have their preferences about the order of the dance. Each dance has its own characteristics and duck dances are no different.

The Seminole of Oklahoma do a lively duck dance. The Nez Perce do a duck and dive version of the duck dance. This is a warrior dance that is a reenactment of a battle. The Chippewa, the Creeks, Caddos, and several pueblos hold duck dances. Many other tribes do duck dances as well. The music for each dance is unique, drumming and singing often accompanied by flute music. Duck dances are great fun so they probably won't go out of style anytime soon.

Duck Clan people speak their truth. They have a way of blurting it out, like it or not. You know what they say when duck people are around: "Duck." We all know that the truth can be sobering. Many people don't like it, but members of the Duck Clan just can't be false, even if they want to be. Ducks are hardwired for veracity, are forthright and stable, have emotional strength, and don't get caught up in drama.

Ducks are about community. They know the power of openness, truth, and like-mindedness. If you feel an attraction to the Duck Clan, say so. Say your truth and you will soon have a straightforward truthful answer in return.

EAGLE

Eagles are the largest raptors—formidable birds of prey. They have hooked beaks and remarkable eyesight. There are two major types of eagles on Turtle Island, golden eagles and bald eagles, usually found in the same areas. Other eagles found on this continent migrated from Asia and Eurasia.

Any way you cut it, the eagle is the chief of all birds. Eagles know and understand the highest spiritual realms and golden eagles are known as the guardians of the east. Eagles have perfect awareness and project an effortless, timeless love and understanding. They are loyal, free-spirited, and independent. They hold the maximum of spiritual authority. If you hang with the eagle, you will find enlightenment—so it has been spoken by the great chiefs since the dawn of time. Eagle was flying in the above world long before there were religions.

Eagle is the spirit of touching and seeing and knowing, a holy warrior informed by truth. Eagles fly near the sun and are related to the sun and the sun's children, those spirit beings embracing the sun, the souls of great warriors, and of women who have died in childbirth.

The spiritually awakened eagles fly close to the Great Mystery in the highest of upper world territories. They are expansive, brave, and regal. Eagle Clan people are beyond the mundane because they have reached for the heavens. They can soar high above all earthly difficulties.

Members of this clan rise on the wings of their soul. They have a huge spherical aura that surrounds them. Eagle people are the embodiment of valor. They are fearless and never petty. They have courage and high warrior power and embody fierceness with dignity. They are spiritual, yet down to earth and engaging. They present a wide vision of the world and know the eternal mysteries.

Inside the Eagle Clan, one is aligned with the healing powers of the eagle and an inner spiritual guidance pushing one toward illumination. The clear-sightedness of the eagle is the keenest vision of all, eyes that see everything, the overt and the concealed, eyes that see the spirit in spirit. The high-warrior eagle is a great magician—bold and creative in thought, word, and deed. People in the Eagle Clan are at the apex of self-discovery and self-knowledge and this is the reason why one may be drawn to the eagle's elucidation.

If you are of the Eagle Clan, you are blessed with many positive attributes. The eagle brings light and holiness to assist humanity.

ELK

Elk are known as the great and commanding *wapiti*, as they are called in the Lakota language, a name now used by many tribes. An exact translation of *wapiti* would be a light-colored deer.

Elk are members of the deer tribe. However, they are much larger than deer. Elk are huge—seven feet at the shoulders. Elk's antlers are huge too, like the open hands of a giant with fingers pointing at the sky. Elk are not fully developed until their fourteenth year. The color of the animal is dark brown with a yellowish hue. They are larger than life and impressive.

Elk Clan people are impressive too. Their movements are lithe and even. They are masters of pacing, of timing, of perfect pitch. Better pacing makes life flow more easily. Think of elk as long-distance runners. They don't stop. They endure. They have strength, power, and stamina. They are a lesson in self-management. They teach you to have goals and how best to use your energy to accomplish them. Theirs is a message of empowerment and confidence. Carry an elk tooth for endurance and blessings.

The Elk Clan way teaches you to be ever so careful, not to rush headlong into a situation just because it looks good. Elk instruct you to do your due diligence. They are goal oriented and counsel you to persevere carefully and pay attention to your inner knowing. Seek the high ground and make sure it is the right, perfect timing for you to participate. You will have all the drive and energy you will need.

There are some few Native American male elk dancers, usually dancing to the accompaniment of an elk whistle or shrill fluting, who are said to be able to call women to them irresistibly. Elk medicine men do know many love medicines, so it is told. There are arguments still current about whether or not it is ethical to use elk power in this manner. Needless to say elk medicine keepers were, and still are, sought after by many a lovesick male.

The first meeting of all the clans was presided over by an elk chief and to this day, all clans can profit from elk's guidance. The Elk Chief counseled the clans to stay close, to abide by their traditions and ceremonies, to keep their clan stories alive. And when they have serious differences of opinion, to work them out in good council. Finally, the clan should always honor the clan mother.

The elk is a symbol of plenty. If this is your clan, all your needs—physical, mental, and spiritual—can be met by mastering pacing and timing. Elk Clan people have big mountain spirits as allies. They have nobility, pride, and self-respect and they are in it for the long spiritual trek that leads to completion.

FIRE

Fire converts the energy of fuel into various other forms such as heat, smoke, ash, and light. In order to exist, fire must devour some other element. It has to be active. If there is a lot of food for a fire within reach, fire will eat it. If it is deprived of food, it will extinguish itself. Differing from the other primary elements, which are fixed and constant, fire is a glutton that it feasts when it can.

Members of the Fire Clan have warmth aplenty. They are fearless. They can make it hot for just about anyone. They live with passion. They are quick to anger. They can turn from smoldering embers into a conflagration. They have hasty minds and because of this fast-moving mental ability, they can leap to conclusions. They have an opinion about everyone and everything.

These people love excitement and seek it out. They are ardent. They are doers. As often as not, they are charismatic. They may be overpoweringly so. Sometimes they are too much and burn weaker people out. Their inner fire can consume and destroy or it can bring warmth and light. It is a clan of great paradox.

Magic belongs to the fire—so say Fire Clan members. They have mastery over heat. They walk on burning coals. They are the fire handlers. They blow fiery breaths on patients during healing ceremonies. Fire people say they know how to keep themselves dry and can burst into flames at will. They fly through the night sky as fireballs. It is their preferred method of travel when visiting other clan members.

There are thousands of myths of how fire came to be in the possession of humans. In most myths it was stolen from gods, extraterrestrials, other godlike beings, or even from a terrifying dragon or other monster. Owning fire, survival was assured.

As a rule, people need the energy of fire in its physical form, for heat, for protection, and so forth. People similarly need inner alchemical fires—the fires of the heart and the fires of the mind. But this element, fire, always needs to be in balance. You don't build a fire without making boundaries so it can be contained. Fire can be explosive and get out of control. Fire can leap and spread and cause untold destruction. Fire energy requires respect. In one fire ceremony a person holds a flaming stick to be released to the sacred fire of the people. As it is let go, attachments and undesirable energies are also released. There is a bit of fire in earth, air, and water—a constant that permeates the universe. It is the spirit at the heart of all matter.

If you think you are of the Fire Clan, you will need to know that you can stand the heat, that you can play with fire and get away with it. The Fire Clan will help you expand and rekindle your passion for life and spike your creativity. Warm your spirit in flames; the Fire Clan furnishes a crucible to transform and mold a new life of spirit and accomplishment.

FISH

Fish are cold-blooded, limbless, vertebrate creatures with gills and fins. The sweeping movement of their tail propels them through the water admirably. Their fins are used as balancers and can be applied as breaks to their forward momentum.

Fish are highly sensitive and their life is lived in water—a hypersensitive medium. Fish were the first astronomers and astrologers, that is to say they observed what was reflected on the surface of the water, as well as the sky and the sky's turning. They know the sun, moon, and stars, the heavens, and the deepest of the murky deep. Fish have been respected and considered sacred all over the world in times past.

Fish know the secrets of water. Water contains numerous mysterious powers. Fish are silent yet they know the songs the water sings and orient themselves by what it is singing in each moment. With water as their medium, fish swim through our unconscious and play at the edges of waterborne lost memories.

There are many fish clans, including old sockeye salmon, silver chub, green sturgeon, shad, dogfish, (Johnny) darter, bullhead catfish, pike, white perch, gar, carp, black bass, sunfish, bull trout and brook trout, and many others— even merman and mermaid clans. These fish, because of their individual merits, have all been the hallmark of well-established clans at one time or another. Various of these clans held fish dances at the appropriate times.

Fish Clan people have the highest intelligence. They are known for their propensity for meditation and scholarly pursuits. They are philosophers, judges, teachers, and in bygone times they were hunters, warriors, and peace chiefs with knowledge of how to resolve disputes. They are natural leaders. They are wise elders who grow bald and live to a very old age. Members of the Fish Clan tend to be idealists, seers, and visionaries. Some are said to have the power to shapeshift or even be in several places at once. They know their ancestors emerged from the sea.

If you feel this is your clan and you are a soothsayer or stargazer, you can call to the hidden fish of the waters to help in realizing your clan. Pray on the shores of a river, lake, or ocean. Pray to the fish spirits. Pray a prayer to the good spirits of the deep for healing and blessing. Try to feel their energy comforting and balancing you. If these are your guiding ancestor spirits, your prayers will soon be answered.

FLINT

Stones represent and symbolize a variety of characteristics. Stones are solid, strong, and patient. Flint is a hard sedentary stone related to quartz. It is usually gray to dark gray and may have a glossy appearance. Flint is plentiful on the North American continent and was used by early inhabitants to make arrowheads, hatchets, and other tools that were used in hunting and warfare. These weapons with their cutting potential date back to antiquity.

Flint is carried for protection and to reverse shyness—often in the form of an arrowhead. This fosters psychological strength to stand your ground in confrontations and arguments. Intellect becomes their weapon, cold and cutting, like flint. Flint carried as a talisman also sharpens mental ability. A flint knife can be used on the spirit plains to cut away from bad relationships and unscrupulous people. In short, used in ritual, it will sever those negative emotional ties that bind.

On other metaphysical levels, a flint knife has been used for psychic surgery, and in olden times, medicine people used flint to perform operations. Flint assists in every sort of separation ritual. It has also been used as an aid in thought projection and to enhance the ability to receive other people's thoughts as well as thoughts from other realms. Flint is a symbol for protection, defense, force, movement, power, and is used as a guide for direction of travel. When given to another person, it is thought to cement a friendship.

Members of the Flint Clan are emotionally stable. The sacred fire sparks from them just as it does when flint is used to strike against pyrite—to cause sparks on tinder and start a fire. Flint Clan people have cut through discordant energy and are optimistic. They are often financial geniuses.

Flint Clan people are down to earth and honest. They will help you cut away sluggish energy. They have the hunter instinct. They are alert to all forms of deception and know when someone is lying to them. They don't get sucked in. They become aloof and keep a good distance from a liar while holding a strong grasp of the truth.

At one time in the forgotten past, the Flint Clan was a military clan. The virtues of the clan are countless. They are a profoundly spiritual clan that has transited the generations. They have inner peace through their rock-hard strength. The Flint Clan has always stood against the forces of destruction and darkness. To become a member, you are scratched and swear allegiance while holding a warrior's flint axe.

FLUTE

Flutes are open tubes that air is blown into to produce high-pitched sounds. They are among the oldest of the wind way musical instruments. Different cultures the world over tootle a flute. Some ancient flutes were made of bone. Some were made of ivory, glass, and even metal and plastic. The flute is a very popular instrument and is used in every genre of music from pop to classical. There is a great variation in the kinds and qualities of flutes in Native America. Flutes are mostly wooden but some are clay. Flutes have been used by shamans since time immemorial to produce power sounds to alter consciousness.

Listening to flute music can open your heart and mind. The flute is important in many spiritual and mystical traditions. Krishna played the flute. The god Pan danced over fields while playing the flute. It is taught that the right flute at the right time can wake up the chakras with the correct and appropriate sounds. Flute music can enlighten you. The flute is still used in Turkey today to accompany the transcendent whirling of the dervishes.

Flute Clan people are accomplished musicians and know how to pipe enticing, luring, enchanting sounds that will transport you to other times and other places. Members of the Flute Clan are often mad with happiness. They are in touch with singing birds, the shrill wind, the sounds emitted by green plants, and blooming plants. They are always aware of the musical spheres and the sacredness of the moment.

Clan members may be dreamers, poets, visionaries, or musicologists. The may rap or rock or kick out some sludge metal. They could just as easily play in a symphony orchestra or a garage band. They are in touch with the lower world and informed with knowledge of the deep self, harmony, happiness, and prosperity. They know how to call the muses and attain those elusive musical qualities that sync one with magic.

Music lives in their heart, the little boneflute girl and the little boneflute boy. They are pied pipers keeping the balance of rain, growth, and decay. They court the proper amount of sunshine. Their flute calls the plants to grow and their powerful ceremonies enliven the spirit of all who witness them.

The flute will help you negotiate a spiritual path. Follow the spirits of the flute. If your heart is full of poetry, if you hear the music without hearing it and dance the living dance of the fluting piper, and become one with the great dance of creation, let the music take you to that soul-sound center in the House of Flutes. You will soon be at home in the Flute Clan.

FOREHEAD

The human forehead is thought to be the site of inner and outer transformation. We receive information about the outside world through observation and other sense data. Inner observation is just as important—perhaps the most important. The forehead is the separation point between inner and outer worlds and perceptions of the soul.

Most people divide the world up into different things. Not only that, but we also make judgments about them. "This is good. That's bad." Their eyes don't penetrate the wholeness. There is a lot of confusion about what's what and what we can do about it. Not so with shamans. They do know what to do about it and they have long since done it.

Forehead Clan people are visionaries. They may be highly unconventional. They have shifted their world and penetrated all darkness. They teach spiritual insightfulness and maturity. Their eyes are open gates to Mystery. They see kindred people of the light. They ask you to travel this same road of inner awakening. They are called "Forehead" Clan because their third eye is open.

Members of this clan are often called seers in that they see the world with opened spiritual eyes. They teach that this is the sacred way. They think in positives. Even in the negatives they see the hidden positives. Dualities don't exist for them. It's all good.

The Forehead Clan is a helping, sage, and loving clan. It is said that their eyes have been opened to see past illusion. One can even say they are fused with divine intelligence— many are those whose eyes have revealed to them our connection to the many worlds we inhabit simultaneously.

Members of the Forehead Clan always see the correct road and don't stray far from it. They are never lost.

Forehead Clan people, as they progress on their journey, may initially imagine themselves to be crazy. They feel pressure in their forehead. They may hear voices, experience unusual, unnatural dreams, and so on.

They must pass through that veil. They are the ones who see, who have inner and outer matching realities—enlightenment. They have out-of-body experiences and heightened perceptions. They observe more and can do more than normal people. They see spirits and anomalous beings not of this world.

Members of this clan have excellent intuition, an accurate and higher form of awareness. They are clairvoyant. Their mind has greatly expanded. They can see events in other lands, no matter the distance. A lot of people do not want to see into the future or even into the distance. However, Forehead Clan people must.

Find the Forehead Clan by experiencing union, the mystical experience of knowing your own soul and, by extension, all souls.

This clan teaches an elevated mindfulness, occult knowledge, and supraconsciousness. It is a joining. One discovers this clan not by seeking but by opening. Go to a Forehead Clan person for pragmatic teachings of the spiritual realization of who and what you are.

Not too fast, slowly, slowly, as the masters say.

FRESH LAND

Initially, "fresh land" meant land not covered by water, but long ago it was redefined as areas where there were no human footprints. It means a place of new beginnings, new origins, first traces—standing at the center of a new creation. It means the journey is over and the time to set to work building a better world is at hand.

Every clan has a story. The Fresh Land Clan story is a remembering that we live in a sacred place. From the west, the people followed a signifying "red pole" that led them in a migration to the east. The sacred leaning red pole was also known as the "red stick" or "baton rouge." The divine pole belonged to a prophet, a powerful shaman. When the people camped, the shaman planted the red pole in the ground and tied his medicine bundle to it. The red pole leaned to the east each morning and the people continued in that direction. Finally, after the long journey of many hundreds of miles, the stick remained upright. The people knew they had arrived on the fresh land they were seeking. It became their new homeland.

You won't find any "bring down" artists among the members of the Fresh Land Clan. Fresh Land people smile. They have great attitudes and are positively charged. They are storehouses of good energy that uplifts everyone around them. They have sought and found fresh land to build their dreams upon. They choose to be happy and brilliant. They laugh at adversity and plow through it. They love change and juggle it until it works in their favor. They are good for a laugh and always look to the future for even better things to come. They never complain.

The Fresh Land Clan instructs you to drop judgment and practice awareness. Take a step forward and don't back up. They tell you to be grateful and count your blessings each day. Find joy in the little things, the little medicines in life that we often overlook. If something is the matter, quit sniveling and do something to fix it. Be kind to everyone and be especially kind to animals.

A Fresh Land blessing ceremony takes place in a large circle with blessings to each direction, entering at the east and going to the south, west, and north and back to the east to complete the circle. In each direction the sacred powers pertaining to that direction are acknowledged. It is asked that the people, families, clans, communities, and ultimately, all the beings existing on the Fresh Land be blessed and learn to live in a sacred manner. In this prayer circle each person prays out loud to the Mystery, thankful that everyone's needs are being met.

The Fresh Land Clan holds prayer meetings and ceremonies on bright, sunshiny days because the sun is always forthright and honest, like them. If you are in the Fresh Land Clan, stand tall and keep your head high above the fray. Whistle a happy tune. Touch the earth, touch the fresh land because it is sacred.

FROG

Frogs are amphibious and live on land and in water. They don't drink water, they absorb it through their skin. They have eyes on the top of their head. Their back legs are strong and they can jump a great distance.

Frogs are the best guides through harsh changes. They are slippery and can instantly spring from danger. A frog can get far and away from jeopardy fast. Slippery medicine is not a bad thing to have. If you get too close, the frog jumps in the water.

The singing of frogs fills the night air with romance since their songs are a calling for a mate. Their song also calls the life-giving rain. A certain frog serenade will bring floods or, perhaps more significantly, drought. A frog is a paradox because of its water/earth dualistic nature. When the frog population is happy, there is abundance.

Frogs are a symbol for love and prosperity in many cultures. They can also be magicians and mind readers— watch what you think around frog people. They are widely regarded as resurrection symbols. If you think you can handle these various enigmatic and conflicting frog powers, the clan of the frog may indeed be yours. They dive deep into life's mysteries and their clan is a repository for ancient knowledge. With frog capabilities we can heal ourselves and others and clean up the environment along the way.

Frog Clan people can get a bad rap and they are often said to be black magicians, witches, and warlocks. They are known for their potions, powders, and other mind- altering concoctions. For a price, they will cast spells. Members of this clan can help barren women to conceive and perform many other wonderworks using their powers of sorcery. A frog skin has many magical potentials. It catches elusive sound qualities and can pick up on vibrations and various emotional frequencies. Shamans everywhere use frogs and frog medicines to combat stress and trauma.

Frog people are also associated with the creation of ceremonial water—the waters from different springs infused with differing energies and used for specific purposes. They pray for water and put their good intentions in it. They experience the deep waters of emotion. They are noted medicine carriers for cleansing the world from toxicity—a job that gets bigger and bigger with increased risks from industrial and other lethal wastes. To do this, they are experts on poisons.

Have the times got you down? Are you aghast at environmental degradation? Do you cry over the destruction of ecosystems? Are you tired of breathing air that is a toxic soup and drinking chemicalized water? Are you feeling the need for an emotional cleansing? Perhaps you are feeling the call of the Frog Clan to help in this process. There is no better clan to help you pick up your spirits. Hop to if you feel the call to become a member of the froggiest of clans. You will find this clan somewhere near the water's edge.

GOPHER

Gophers are small furry rodents that use their sharp claws and even their teeth to dig underground. They are continually digging and never seem to finish building their extensive networks of tunnels. They create mounds that can be dangerous to people walking in the area who may well trip or sink into the soft dirt the gophers have dished out. Gophers are voracious eaters and have large fur-lined cheek pouches they use to transport food. They are also notorious hoarders and can stockpile enormous amounts of food.

Gopher Clan people are messengers of the deep earth. They can pull from the earth insights to profound questions. Gophers are shamans. They know the subconscious mind. They know the hidden drives that motivate people. They know how to find your lost memories—sometimes painful and beautiful but repressed. They know how to heal you.

Members of the Gopher Clan are often power doctors with pronounced healing abilities. They are curers. They are wise. They have earth power and earth magic. They know where the buried booty is hidden—pirate booty and even intellectual and spiritual booty. A gopher may share a message with you from the deepest of the deep lower world, and tell you where to dig in order to find that buried treasure.

Gopher Clan people are often the hidden power behind a chief, or in today's dominant world societies, the power behind presidents and kings. They always give advice, good and bad. They have a dark network of friends. Some say gophers have the power to bless and curse, heal and kill. They never lose at gambling. They can "see" into any gambling game and know exactly when and what to bet. They have the edge unless they get unnecessarily greedy, in which case they will soon lose their shirt just like everyone else.

Gopher people like cities and prefer the urban life. They are the insiders. They get information from many sources, including their own intuition. They know how to interpret confounding data. They always have a handle on what is going on. They have good as well as evil powers and will use both as they feel the need. The clan is not easily recognizable, being low key and discreet. If you are drawn to certain people and engage with them and you know they have the mysterious gopher powers you are seeking, you will be admitted into this clan.

GROUSE

Grouse are loners and live out on the prairie tundra. They have solid bodies with short legs. Many have a crest on their head. They have fan-shaped tail feathers and their neck feathers are large. With their plumage, dark browns with variously reddish tones, and their spots and bars, grouse are colorful and attractive. They can often be heard on the cold northern steppes producing a drumming-like sound made by a male wishing to attract a female.

Grouse are sensitive. The male birds are noted for their love cries. In the early springtime when the smell of sage and the clean scent of prairie grasses fill the air, male grouse go a-strutting and a-courting—proud, sure, confident, and a bit bold, colorful with their swelling wattles and their chestnut brown and striped tail feathers bustling.

When confronted with another male, the grouse taunt and attack each other in spirals but it is not so much physical as it is a ritual dance of lust and authority. It is a battle dance, back and forth—a test of will, a true mating dance in the theatre of desire. They peck, they ruffle feathers, they twist and circle one way, then another—a performance most lively. It is a dominance dance that determines which male is the most attractive, the prettiest, the most desirable, and the one best suited for mating. It is an awe-inspiring performance compelled by a longing that is the heart and soul of passion. There is only one winner—well, maybe two.

Later, after these ritual dances are done, you see grouse in pairs—male and female soul bonded. Still later, you see a happy grouse mother with her darling hatchlings trailing behind her.

Members of the Grouse Clan have an immediate presence. They have the appearance of being at the still point in the sphere of the self. A potent energy surrounds them. A constant whirr seems to be in the air when you are near them. Their life force is impossible to ignore.

Grouse Clan people are realized. They love and they are loved. They are in touch with their deepest soul. They live their lives in cycles. They are the always dancers in a circle dance. With each round they accumulate knowledge. They seek wisdom and they find it. They reach for a perfected state within the choreography of existence. The Grouse Clan can take you across stormy seas to the spiritual initiation you seek, a journey to your true center, a journey to the inner light.

HAWK

Hawks are a beautiful family of birds from the goshawk to the sparrow hawk. Like eagles, they are raptors—powerful birds of prey with hooked beaks and sharp talons. They are also divers—catching mice, snakes, and rabbits at a fell swoop. They have unmatched visual skills and see in color. Female hawks are larger than males.

Hawks are sunbirds, masters of the golden rays of the wide, blue, upper world. If you are one of the Hawk Clan people, creative ideas come to you easily from their vast pool of information and experience. You can glide home free. They also furnish perspective. In other words, they can read the times and see how one event fits into another.

Members of the Hawk Clan have sharp, hawk eyes. They hover over problems until they solve them. They are astute observers. They are contemplative and analytical. They don't miss a trick. Hawks have high-minded principles yet they are down to earth.

Listen to them. They are sacred messengers translating messages from the soul of the wind, which knows every-thing. They are brave and beautiful. They are often related in myth and symbol to the afterlife. In ancient Egyptian beliefs, a being with a hawk's head and a human body escorted the dead to paradise. Hawks are said to be the soul of the soul. They are magic birds speaking enlightening words of power to all those who will listen.

Members of the Hawk Clan can be prophetic oracles. If need be, trust your hawkish instincts and strike a blow for personal freedom. Push through. Hawks have strength and power and they overcome obstacles. They will not let their foresight slip away without making the most of it.

Hawk Clan people are also communications experts, knowledgeable and skilled in computer technology, including hacking. They are good traders and can move goods quickly, including information. They may be merchants, travelers, or may work in the travel industry. They are often athletic and love the outdoors. They love adventure and freedom. They may be race car drivers or boat racers. They are transition experts. On the dark side, they can be tricksters and thieves. No matter their morals, they are always eloquent and convincing.

Hawks are often involved with media. They magnify information. They make wonderful investigative reporters and always get the scoop. Some are statisticians. They figure heavily in information technology. To find this clan, hop on your computer and dig.

HOLLY LEAF

There are many varieties of holly—trees, shrubs, vines, and climbers. Holly was used in pagan rites of wintertime, eventually becoming associated with the season of Christmas. Holly leaf with its dark green leaves and red berries is a decorative plant with popping colors.

Holly is slow growing and its habitat ranges from the tropics to frosty cold mountainous terrain. Some common names of holly are mountain holly, cat berry holly, possum holly, horned holly, and sand holly. By and large holly can be a dangerous plant to consume. However, some plants are used to make teas such as Yerba Mate. Most holly is bitter and some can cause nausea and vomiting.

Holly leaf, especially the Ilex vomitoria, also known as yaupon holly leaf, is an emetic. A traditional concoction that included this ingredient was known as black medicine drink. It was often dispensed ceremonially in the early springtime in ceremonies known as "the busk." It was believed to purify the blood and improve eyesight. Drinking the black draft was a detoxification ceremony that removed physical and spiritual contamination. Unwanted entities flee from people who drink the medicine.

There are many steps that must be followed in making the drink. The black beverage is boiled over glowing coals for many hours in a large pot holding several gallons of the potion. The ingredients used in the making of the bitter black medicine drink are highly secret but they included the leaves, stems, and roots of the yaupon holly to which other emetic herbs and undisclosed ingredients were added. The end result is a liquid that induces dry heaves and vomiting similar to the effects of peyote or ayahuasca. The body is rocked with intense paroxysms that can eventually lead to a perfect angelical bliss. You just have to get through the hellish nausea part.

The black medicine drink is known to have given certain people second sight, the ability to see into the future, and other divinatory powers. The drink often spawned telepathic capabilities—a sudden mind link with another person. Birth memories and past life memories were common after drinking the traditional black medicine drink. Taking the medicine is an aid to forgiving others their transgressions and for forgiving our own wrongdoings.

Holly Leaf Clan people are sparse, lean, spare—essential. They are very understated and often have a wistful quality in their gaze. They will teach you many hidden and secret ways to call money and good luck, and to learn the art of dream magic. Their personal space, their environment, reflects their Spartan, minimal lifestyle. To be in this clan, one must be spiritually cleansed, unafraid, accepting, tolerant, and in love with all of life lived in each perfected moment. It is a baptism of sorts—all old selves purged, new selves awakening. It is as though you have been sheltered during the long winter. The rebirth is coming.

Oddly enough, it is the beginning of spring when this clan is most active and visible to spiritual eyes. It is a path to sacredness, healing, and spiritual devotion. Finding this clan is a transforming journey to a heaven on earth. All you have to do is find the right spirit doctor to accompany you there.

HORN

Horn, in this case the buffalo horn, joins one to the heart and spirit of the mighty buffalo, the chief of all the animals. Horn is a symbol for the strength and power that is concentrated in the horn. Even in an old piece of buffalo horn chip there is a radionics—a retained power of the actual buffalo. A buffalo horn talisman, a horn chip, is said to rejuvenate the person who carries it and reawaken divine facets that the individual has lost.

This medicine is not about buy and sell. It is good to support Native American arts and crafts. But there is no honor in buying animal horns, skins, hooves, or other parts. No one should play a part in endangering animals. You must find your own medicines in nature or they should be gifted to you in a good medicine way.

Carrying a small piece of buffalo horn chip unites one with spiritual and physical healing. It frees one from the ties that bind, whatever those bindings are. It opens the way for contact with ancestor spirits and animal spirits—both four-legged and winged. It can wake up a force inside you, a mystery power that touches upon the divine.

The little piece of buffalo horn is a call to spiritual arms and a pledge to share and do service in the community. The buffalo represents prayer and connection to Great Spirit. The great animal signifies generosity and honor. Horn Clan people bring peace to one's soul and core being.

Horn Clan people have a big spirit, yet they are humble. They are prayerful, inspiring, determined people. They are a force united with the earth and with personal freedom. They are a deeply spiritual lot. They seem to make every life they come in contact with better. They have the courage to be honest and don't pretend to be anything other than they are. They are self-sacrificing and united in respect for all things sacred.

Members of this clan may appear a bit stiff and stand-offish but you will find they always get the job done. Today, the buffalo dance is held annually throughout the Great Plains region of Turtle Island. It should be obvious if you are drawn to the Horn Clan. You love your community and want to pitch in. The moment you enter this clan's circle, you feel serenity, peace, and all the love and acceptance you could possibly want.

HORSE

Ancient horses were at first hunted and later domesticated. Horses have evolved over millions of years from a three-toed creature about the size of a sheep and not much resembling the powerful and elegant creatures we know today. Unless they have been mistreated, horses have the sweetest of dispositions. Their spirits can run very high, but still they are affectionate and gentle.

A horse brings the balance needed to make life viable. Horses trample down evil spirits. They respect and honor their clan ancestors. The horse way is the correct way, following the rule of ancient spiritual teachings. They bless the way for every man and woman and gladly bring like-minded people into their great clan. Horses have contributed much to civilization. They have served humankind from time immemorial. Horses are believed to have originated in Central Asia. Now they range the world over. All their celebrations and ceremonies are based on the moon calendar, a calendar of twenty-eight-day cycles.

The universe is said to be a horse and the horse's underbelly is the Milky Way Galaxy, also known as the pathway of human souls. Horses came to earth from the sky. Members of the Horse Clan are sleek, elegant, and exude power and panache. Although, in general, they have a sweet disposition, a few Horse Clan people are hot and quick tempered with emotions stronger than one might think. Most, however, are affectionate and make friends easily. They usually have excellent health, prosperity, and a long and fruitful life. They are possessed with a wonderful energy. They are polished and cultivated in their demeanor. They are spirited gentlepeople. They are exuberant. They can't wait to get into the race, metaphorically speaking.

Horse Clan people are highly sensitive. They hear better. They pick up on subtle energies near and far. They have psychic abilities and read minds. They help others to raise their consciousness. Their energy alone can heal a lost and damaged person—just being near them in the moment restores confidence and lifts spirits.

Horses are social and Horse Clans have principal male and female chiefs. They have a pecking order from the alphas to the lowest ranking member of the clan. Alphas exert a strong influence over the entire group. This is not a bad thing in the face of so many strong personalities. An individual horse's power comes from their place in the group dynamic. All horses are powerful.

Horse people help show others how to restore personal power. That is their specialty. That is their mission. They can appear anywhere in our modern landscape. When you are near them, they automatically recharge your battery, giving you a lift from their energetic presence. Spend time with horses. Bond with them. Feed them an apple and some carrots. Take the reins. And you will realize your personal power is returning. By helping this great being, you have helped yourself.

You know you are Horse Clan if your spirit calls you to value movement, courage, integrity, and freedom. You are Horse Clan if you are concerned with your herd, with their survival, safety, and well-being. You are Horse Clan if hold your head high and look into the face of danger to protect others. You are Horse Clan if an ancient voice speaks to you about the wild nature of your humanity and about the connectedness of all living beings. Horse Clan people have deep inner knowledge of the great giveaway for others.

HUMMINGBIRD

Hummingbirds are the smallest birds. You hear their whirr but you don't see their wings—they are moving too fast, about two hundred wing strokes per second. Hummingbirds have great memories and recall each flower they visit. They see and hear better than humans. Hummingbirds gravitate to their favorite color, red.

The hummingbird is a symbol for great joy and happiness. If you must move from a negative situation in life, hummingbird will help you to do it. Hummingbirds furnish the primordial spark to source the fires of your freedom. It doesn't matter if the move is around the block or thousands of miles away. They will understand and respond quickly to your needs. Let the good and noble spirit of these little creatures guide you in how to get where you want and need to be. They will lead you to your new home.

In day-to-day life, hummingbird can show you the easiest and sweetest road to follow. Members of the Hummingbird Clan are counselors of the heart—creating circles of lovingkindness. If this is your way, you will have a happy life and be an inspiration to others. Live joyfully now. Your energy field will bless others with that selfsame joy.

Hummingbird people are possessed with loving, healing energy. They dance and soar to a higher vibration. They are courageous. Their energy and their lightness of being awaken the medicine flowers. They are known for their independence and loving ways. They are never negative and they lift energy wherever they go. They are warriors and they are never afraid. If necessary, they become ferocious fighters and will defend one of their own to their death.

The Hummingbird Clan tells you to transcend your small self and become the answer to your own questions—to step into the multihued light and become a happy recipient of the highest vibration you are capable of receiving. The hummingbird road is the sweet way and offers ultimate beauty.

Hummingbirds are found solely in the Western Hemisphere. To find the hummingbird spirit, spend time in gardens rife with gorgeous blooming flowers, especially red ones. A garden filled with hovering hummingbirds is music to the ears. Seek the highest vibration and drink in the nectar of change. Follow your bliss, as the slogan goes, for bliss is with the Hummingbird Clan. The clan is highly protective of one another and yet has a healthy love and respect for everyone. It is a high transformation to be sure to become a member of the Hummingbird Clan.

KINGFISHER

Kingfishers are small- to medium-sized, brilliantly colored birds with stubby legs and daggerlike harpoon-shaped bills. The kingfisher sings not at all but does whistle. Though they are called "kingfishers" not all of them eat fish. Those that do eat a dozen or more minnows a day along with a range of aquatic insects, and if you have a fish pond, probably your goldfish.

Kingfishers are a symbol for pure water—water being their chief element. In nature they are said to be able to smooth the surface of a boiling sea. They denote a period of intellectual and spiritual concerns. Kingfishers will help you to let go of repetitive emotional issues and encourage you to forgive yourself over any past failures. They assure that love will soon appear, unfolding beautifully and in sur- prising ways.

Kingfisher Clan people are remarkably beautiful people. Powder blue is their color. They usually live near water and are happy in their marriages or relationships. If they happen to be single, they are content with that. Along with glowing skin, pleasing dress, and charming manners, they are bril- liant conversationalists. They do not tolerate coarseness or inappropriate speech. They have a contagious calmness and never lose their cool. They have inner peace and live a refined life of abundance and prosperity. They are also lucky and always attract good fortune.

The Kingfisher Clan will teach you how to defeat nega- tivity and live a life of serenity. These fishers of knowledge point the way to graciousness and beauty. If Kingfisher Clan is your direction, you will shoot through the status quo and find spiritual unity. Kingfisher teachings are full with holiness and tradition.

Make no mistake. The kingfisher bird is a medicine bird. There are hundreds of stories about the kingfisher leading sick people to a lake, stream, or spring and submerging them in the water. This act would clean septic wounds and heal all manner of illnesses. Ask kingfisher to take you to the spirit waters and the medicine waters, the invigorating waters generating strong life and well-being.

The Kingfisher Clan offers a lantern of light in times of darkness. Its members are active and always engaged in some sort of project. Whether it is to raise money for athletes or to beautify a neighborhood, they are always occupied. They also offer the very best techniques to help you with past life issues, especially past life karma where you may have abused power, or a lifetime where you may have joined with hidden dark forces bent on doing harm to others. They know ceremonies that will lessen or completely eradicate bad karma and help you achieve an inner cleansing and enjoy the fruits of being in this clan.

KIT FOX

Kit foxes make their homes in the southwestern deserts. There is also a high population of kit foxes in Mexico. They are nocturnal but are occasionally seen in the day. They have a large head and large scoop-like ears that are close together. They have excellent hearing. They are gray in color with a black-tipped tail. Kit foxes eat small animals, including rabbits, mice, rats, and even squirrels. They don't have to drink much water to survive because they get enough liquid from their kills.

Kit Fox Clan people are astute. They are agile, cunning, and adaptable to any situation. They are independent. They are masters of the terrain. They have the power to blend in and become invisible. They walk the land without being known or seen. They have been called shapeshifters by indigenous cultures the world over.

There are countless old love tales of beautiful women and handsome men who were actually kit foxes. The basic story goes something like this: A woman walking in a field sees a male fox. The two gaze into each other's eyes. A powerful energy is passed between them. The woman approaches and the fox bounds away. A few days later, there's a knock on the door. The woman opens it to find the most handsome man she has ever seen. He says he is lost and needs help. She asks him in for a cuppa. They talk. They laugh. He stays over.

The two live happily together, but after a few weeks, up jumps a tragic flaw. He often goes missing at night. He has any number of excuses. She gets suspicious and follows him and discovers he is a fox. She is brokenhearted. In one

ending he disappears, leaving her to contemplate her wonderful experience with an animal. Of course, this plot has
many other endings, none of them all that happy.

As you can see, kit foxes are unusual animals. They can
be soul searchers, specializing in healing soul loss and in soul
reclamation. They have taught their clan ways and means to
seek souls in trauma and return them to their original own-
ers, restoring them to sound mental and physical health.

Members of the Kit Fox Clan lead their kin to health
and well-being. They know the good spirits they are looking for so they are able to seize them when they appear.
Kit foxes have various rare shamanic gifts. They have always
facilitated communication between the living and the dead.
When the way is unclear to others, the kit fox knows full
well how to read the signs concerning what lies ahead.

The kit fox is very much a trickster, similar to the coyote
though not so coyote-shameful. Unlike the coyote, the kit
fox doesn't fall for his own machinations. Coyote is invari-
ably his own victim. Kit foxes never get caught in the traps
they have set for others. And the traps they set never fail.
Let a kit fox show you how to slip away unseen from any
number of dangerous situations. Many Kit Fox Clan people
are magicians of the highest distinction. If they are calling to
you from other plains not of this earth and you get the message, follow it. Kit foxes are the most difficult animal there
is to track—they walk in invisibility. Let them find a kindred
spirit—you.

LIZARD

These fun and elegant creatures are reptiles. They have scales, sharp teeth, and claws. Most of them are quick and spontaneous. There are many types of lizards from the gecko to the Komodo dragon—small as a finger up to a size larger than a human being.

Lizards live in all sorts of environments, from the upper elevations of the mountains to low valley areas, from lush forests to sweltering deserts. The only place that does not have a lizard population is Antarctica. They often live in trees and are great climbers. Those living on the ground can be found in near-inaccessible places and every kind of terrain while others will bask in the sun on a city sidewalk.

They can suddenly come out of a dream stupor and streak to another safer spot. Some can run, leap, and catch hold of a twig and then scurry up a tree. In all these locations they can be seen darting about. They live in the borderlands, between hard-core nature and other more ephemeral states.

Lizard Clan people are mystic dreamers and they preside over vision quests, ceremonies that call in spirits, séances, and other sacred rites that link one with the spirit world where any and all realities are possible. Visionary states and dreams are similar. Humans are on one side of the dream while lizards are on the other, a place where all creatures' dreams are revealed. Dreams are lizard's ordinary reality. Even when awake they are dreaming.

Members of the clan go in and out of dream states collectively and individually and believe that dream masters are dreaming our current reality. Some shamans say that bad dreams are sent by a stingy, evil witch and her partner, an equally evil warlock. They eat the dreams of others and make them their own, trying to devour the dreamer's soul. However, it is the love that pervades the cosmos that wins in the end. If you encounter a lizard, hold fast to your dreams. For lizards, the dream is real, much beyond ordinary perceptions, beyond lucid dreaming, and superseding all other realities, merging into one great hyperreality where lizards become Source and are at one with the Absolute.

Dreaming is a discipline that dreamers learn over time. Dreams lead to liberation. The Lizard Clan teaches you to make your dreams your own and not get them confused with dreams that belong to others. Follow the lizard trail into the dreamtime where the lizard dreamers dwell. You will want to start by keeping a dream journal and recording the quality and quantity of your dreams. All your dream experience is important. Lizards move through many worlds, inner and outer. If you are able to follow the mystical guidance hidden inside the dreams of the dreaming Lizard Clan, it will lead you to them. Most spiritual disciplines tell you to wake up. This clan, however, tells you to go to sleep and dream. Wake up inside the dream and there you will find your clan.

To wake up to the possible, dream.

MOLE

Moles are small mammals that can be found the world over except for South America and Antarctica, and in any environment where it is suitable to dig tunnels. They have a cylindrical body, soft dark fur, very small eyes and ears, shortened back limbs, and powerful forelimbs with paws that are perfect for digging.

Moles are the original subterraneans. They are highly sensitive and can teach you how to find hidden parts of yourself—your secret buried past life memories. They will tell you to explore inward. If necessary, they will take you by the hand and lead you there to gaze in the dark mirror. They are able to turn a blind eye on your faults, and to a Mole Clan person your faults might even be considered virtues. Mole Clan people are hypersensitive. They have strong intuitions and are rarely wrong in their judgments.

The mole burrows underground and knows inner earth secrets—the lower regions that are associated with fear and death. The mole is often called Underground Old Man. Down is the direction. Black is the color. Earth is the element. They go deep. They know of hidden treasures, precious stones, healing medicine roots, and in blindness they know light. They are the lower world guardians of every path and they protect the geometry of all directions.

Members of the Mole Clan are difficult to gauge. They are earthy, cautious, secretive, and can even be standoffish. They value privacy. A Mole Clan person makes no public acknowledgment of another clan member. Their expression is blank while in their presence and they show no recognition.

Like the seers of old, the Mole Clan has their appropriate rites and ceremonies in the silence of a dark and hidden cave. No outside energies penetrate the embracing walls. They are able to astral travel to distant locations and communicate with sages and holy people who have renounced the world. During their ceremonies they are able to bond with light beings in other dimensions. Members of this clan are much beyond the material world and manifest their simple needs easily. They have incarnated here on our planet to help suffering humanity. They are the people you don't find on social media. They are more likely to be grubbing in a garden or living some sort of simple utopian lifestyle.

If you are drawn to the Mole Clan and its teachings, construct an earth altar. It should be built outdoors facing west. It should be a small rectangle constructed with a layer of dirt obtained from around a mole burrow. Use prayer sticks, tobacco ties, stones, or any objects that have spiritual meaning for you to empower your altar. These altars connect one to the lower world. Some people wear a small leather pouch of mole dirt as a necklace, a sort of mole oracle that will keep you on your path and lead you to the Mole Clan. The way of the mole is the way of humility and renunciation. It is a way that cannot be opposed.

MOON

The moon, our nearest celestial neighbor, is a natural satellite of the earth and the two are energetically entwined. The moon effects the tides, the seasons, and strange behavior in human interactions. We see only one face of the moon. Half the moon is hidden from view. The moon has magical powers. It makes us receptive to new ideas and practices.

The saliva that the moon emits, the dew, contains a compound that fosters fertility and frightens away bad spirits, keeping them locked in their place. Dew makes the vegetation comfortable and healthy. And so with the trees. How trees react to the dew helps shamans know from which direction sickness comes. Dew is a balancing factor and a necessity for a vigorous life.

On dark nights when the full moon is up in frothy grandeur, you can see the man in the moon, the woman in the moon, and perhaps even the rabbit in the moon, and if you look hard enough, there is also a toad in the many-faced moon. Some people say they see dogs, cats, and even cows in the moon. The moon is witchy, feminine. The moon is strictly about women and female energy. The moon is nurturing. Self-knowledge is impossible without the reflective powers of the moon.

Moon Clan people are often emotive and have intense shifting feelings. They have an inner light that is near blinding. They are guided by this inner light. Other people can be confused and lost—not Moon Clan people. They are honest with themselves in matters of the heart. They are forthright in business. They have learned to cope and not be overwhelmed with mental stress.

When the moon looms large in the night sky, and it is bright, round, and beautiful, Moon Clan gatherings are held. They are often accompanied with ritual music and ceremony, dancing and singing, and are held at the new moon as well as the full moon.

There are thirteen Grandmother Moons in a lunar year. The twenty-eight-day months have picturesque names such as Strawberry Moon, Flower Moon, Sturgeon Moon, Long Night Moon, and hundreds of more names depending on the tribes using them. The Grandmother Moon helps you with your dreams and brings forth visions. If you are drawn to one of the animal clans, pay attention to the moon. The moon has a special relationship with nocturnal animals such as owl and wolf, and may furnish a key to unlock this relationship. If possible, spend time near the ocean meditating on a moon-bright night. Ask the tides for clarity. Let the magnetic pull take you to the Moon Clan. Revitalize your biorhythms. Expect surprises, new comforts, and a remembering of the old way and the old lost magic.

MORNING

The birth of a new day begins with sunrise and gives us our first blessings. The light is new and fresh. Nothing is compromised. Morning gives the promise of purity and a belief in our own abilities. It is a time for trust in existence, a time to realize and claim our spiritual gifts. It symbolizes a wakeup call on many levels.

Morning Clan people are pure of heart and have a thirst for life. Daybreak sun feeds the human spirit. A smudge of sage smoke and prayers at sunrise are not unfamiliar to Morning Clan people. They assemble before sunup. A new day begins, new hope, new promise. A sunrise ceremony might include a song of greeting beginning as the first sunrays appear in the east.

Some Morning Clan ceremonies on important clan dates begin with a dance of women painted chalky white. The dancers have colorful crowned headdresses. They are solemn and the leader of the dance procession sprinkles cattail pollen to her left and right. When the pollen touches the ground, it wakes up deep water energies in the earth that harmonize the vibrations of earth, air, fire, and water.

The dances may go on until late in the day. They symbolize change within and bless the dancers and clan members with strength and virtue and furnish participants with new life-giving power. They are able to heal people at a distance by prayer and projection of this daybreak energy.

Morning Clan members will get up before dawn. You too must rise early if you want to belong to the Morning Clan, and you surely know if this is so by now. They are the women and men of the dawn. They are happy and active.

They are open to insights. They are persistent and unfatigued as the day goes on. They have little anxiety and a high tolerance against stress. They will tell you to rise early, while it is still dark outside and get going. Benjamin Franklin famously said, "Early to bed, early to rise, makes a man healthy, wealthy, and wise." Presumably, he included women in this aphorism. He also said, "The early morning has gold in its mouth." Morning Clan people would agree with these precepts. Your life becomes one big shout, one great big good morning!

MOUNTAIN GOAT

Mountain goats are not really goats. They are more closely related to antelope. They are wooly and white. With their beards, they look wise—like gurus of the high mountains. Their habitat can exceed elevations of thirteen thousand feet. They migrate to a lower elevation in the winter. Mountain goats can get testy when they think their territory is being invaded.

Mountain goats have rings on their dark horns—one less than their age. For example, if they have four rings they are three years old. Female's horns have a curve at the tip while males have a slight bow the entire length of their horns. Regardless of gender, their horns continue to grow throughout their lives.

Members of the Mountain Goat Clan are the strong ones, the surefooted ones, the ones who have made the climb and are confident in their abilities. They are edgy; that is to say, they live a life near the rim rock on the edge of the terrifying abyss. There they do their perilous dance daily in difficult terrain. They are independent yet loyal. They have strong personal ethics and strive to reach the crown of the mountain. They climb forward strategically pushing for the top. They always seek the highest of the high ground and once they have met the test, they reach it.

Mountain Goat Clan people own the mountain. They are respectful of the mountain's grandeur. They make prayers asking the mountain for protection, healing, and wisdom. They constantly commune with the mountain and mountain spirits.

Many people from this clan retire after a successful life in business, having reached the heights of business achievement. If you are attempting any commercial enter-prise, they are the best counselors to go to for advice. They have the logic and instinct for effective commerce. They are adepts and they stand upon a mountain of practical experience. They have given the best of themselves to their occupation through their striving. With their mind and their heart, they are at one with the mountain. They have become the mountain they were once climbing.

If you are determined to ascend a mountain, the Mountain Goat Clan is the clan for you. If you have the gumption, agility, ambition, and if you are driven to stand upon the heights and peer down upon those below you, you are one of those tenacious rare souls who have earned Olympus and deserve immortality.

MOUNTAIN LION

Mountain lions are known by many names. They are called cougar, tiger, catamount, puma, panther, and American lion, just to name a few. They all add up to the same big cat—the largest in North America. The female is about two-thirds the size of the male and can be just as ferocious. Their eyes are a sunny citrine color with vertical pupils. When those eyes spike you, you know you are in the presence of a most imposing being. You know it's time to go—and fast.

Mountain lions go it alone most of the time when searching for food. They are territorial. They are masters of the art of stalking. They like to kill and eat mammals, the larger the better. They are independent, solitary night hunters searching for prey. They usually find it—moose, deer, elk, and very occasionally, domestic cattle. They also eat smaller game such as raccoons, mice, squirrels, and rabbits. They can weigh up to two hundred and twenty pounds, yet they are lithe and powerful and can jump a long distance. They are formidable hunters and often have deer on the menu. They have excellent vision and take in much about you at a glance.

Mountain lions are in a dance with the sun. The sun is the beating heart of our planetary system. Even in the deep of night the mountain lion is feeling the sun on the other side of the world. Their golden color denotes a closeness to the sun.

Mountain Lion Clan people don't say a lot. They exude personal power and are protective of their interests, but they are quietly charismatic. They are courageous, authoritative, and prudent. They are generous and loving. They are centered in their heart. They are a potent force. They are one with their purpose and they get very annoyed with breaks in concentration.

Members of this clan are always in command and they know it. Mountain lion women can see into men's true intentions. They don't play around. They demand honesty and justice. They are also masters of energy. They know how to conserve it and, when necessary, use it. They can pounce with terrible effect and explode in ferociousness, but most of the time, unless they are being threatened, they would rather play it cool.

Most mountain lions have achieved positions of authority. They are in charge. They automatically take responsibility for all the people under them. They look for constructive solutions to problems. They are decisive and make their decisions based on the needs of all concerned. They are magnanimous in their praise and never beat their own chests or seek glory from their actions. If they seek glory at all, it is for their organization or group.

If you have had an empowering vision at the crest of a great mountain, surely this is your calling, your clan. If you think you can handle it, call on a Mountain Lion Clan person to bring you aboard. Or, if you must play follow the leader, there is no better leader to follow than a member of the Mountain Lion Clan.

MOUSE

Mice are thought of as cute little creatures with a long tail, a somewhat long snout, large ears for their size, and beady black eyes. For the most part, they go about their business silent and unseen. They are highly adaptable and can survive in a variety of habitats..They are fastidious in their habits. Mouse teaches that the little details in life are important. Disorder that might be easily overlooked is glaring to mice. A mouse sees the obvious flaws wherever they go; plus they are always discovering new imperfections. Mouse Clan people are intense.

On the other hand, the mouse teaches us to appreciate all of our everyday life experiences. They tell us to savor each step of life's journey—meanwhile keeping an eye out for cats. Each day is a miraculous gift. Give it your best shot, your complete attention. Life is truly a walk in a sacred garden, each moment a unique opportunity to engage with your entire being with rapt attention.

Members of the Mouse Clan, although a bit timid, are diligent, soulful, attentive, and eager to please. When push comes to shove, they will jump. They have a pronounced social nature. They promote get-togethers, dances, prayer meetings, and drumming circles. They have curiosity, endurance, and forbearance. They are adaptable. Mouse councils you to open your eyes, take a serious look at your environment, and seek out the meaning of what appears in your path. Pay attention. Use all your senses. Perhaps get your inner Sherlock Holmes going. Examine closely and seek overlooked meanings and possibilities in ordinary things.

Follow the clues to see if it will lead you to some spiritual cheese.

The master spirit of the mouse is called upon in various healing ceremonies. The shaman uses the mouse spirit to find important factors that have been overlooked concerning their patient. It is felt that nothing can escape mouse's attention. The mouse often suggests the perfect cure or remedy needed.

Mouse Clan people deal with the little necessary matters of great consequence like keeping records and paying taxes. Their message is to clean it up, fix it up, and get the order and numbers straight—to keep the little things shined up and shipshape. If this busywork is your sort of business, you enjoy doing it, and you believe the rest will take care of itself, you should count yourself among these service-minded people as a member of their clan.

One sure message from the Mouse Clan is to squeak up when you don't like something and always sweat the small stuff.

OAK

Long-lived, wise, expansive, boss trees, oaks need a lot of space. They may vary in size, depending on the climate and soil, but can reach a height of over seventy feet, with their branches stretching out a hundred feet. That requires tremendous power and strength and because of their large size, oak trees need a lot of water—fifty gallons a day or more.

The oak is the most majestic and honored of trees. A living oak is a chief tree, a symbol for endurance, courage, and strength. It furnishes a sheltering canopy for spiritual seekers. Great gatherings are held around this tree. The ancients called the oak tree the oracle tree. And indeed, prophetic visions and realizations have occurred at the sturdy base of this teacher tree, a place of sudden insight and spiritual understanding.

Oak Clan people live long and are said to have endurance. They have patience and their spirit triumphs over all obstacles. Their presence is noble. They are connected to many worlds within and without. The Oak Clan is a life-affirming clan. Between two ancient oak trees is an entranceway to ethereal planes—to places of power and unlimited potential. Oak Clan people have passed through this doorway. They often hold their meetings under the stately boughs of this immense tree.

Some Oak Clan teachings concern longevity, stamina, protection, good health, liberation, wisdom, and constancy. Think of a tiny acorn with so much potential, so much to offer in a nutshell. The acorn symbolizes rebirth, reemergence into life and substance, prosperity, and generosity.

Acorns are the fruit of the oak tree. Production starts at twenty to fifty years of age.

Members of the Oak Clan are tenacious like the oak leaf that holds to the tree through the winter. New growth pushes the old leaves from the limbs—a teaching to continually grow so we can let go of old habits.

These people are strong with a long life expectancy. The oak tree is associated with Jupiter, the luck bringer in Western astrology. Oak Clan people are similarly generous. They are philosophers, theologians, skilled social workers, judges, and people who exhibit the wisdom and stability of the oak.

Let the oak tree reconnect you to your soul force, your first self, your original self, to a complete trust in being. Be rooted like the oak tree. Be like the flowering tree of the people. Carry an oak leaf or an acorn for luck or just to absorb the compressed energy of the oak tree. Open the oak door and enter if this is your clan.

OPOSSUM

Opossum are adaptable and effective scavengers about the size of a house cat. They have grayish fur and a white face. They have dark eyes and their ears are hairless; so is their tail. Opossum are mainly found in the eastern half of the United States and in Central America. Opossum build their own dens and they go out and hunt for food at night. They are Turtle Island's only marsupial.

Opossum Clan people are full of guile but you would never know it. Their nature is always to use subterfuge. They are the hidden people, people who have tucked their real identity safely away from sight. They are a charade, a make-believe, a manufacture. They mean no harm by it. It's a defense. They want to protect their true selves and true feelings at all costs because they are hypersensitive. As long as their inner truth is hidden, no one can hurt them. Because of this they are good listeners with a way of not saying much and flipping any discussion back to you.

Members of the Opossum Clan are secretive. Nobody knows for sure who or what they are. They could be your best buddy or that elderly lady living down the block. They could be your banker, your baker, or a bricklayer. They are in disguise and putting on an act—pretending to be some-one they are not. And who they "are not" is who they "are." That is the way of the opossum and the way of the Opossum Clan. And if these possums play it right, no one can criticize or bash them because they are not themselves. There is only an artificiality to bash.

To be a part of the Opossum Clan, you have to fake it. You have to understand the phony within yourself in order to project it and use it to your advantage. That is the only way you can enter and be initiated into their clan, because once you learn their secrets, you can never go back. You must perfect the synthetic you, the you that is not you. You must deceive everyone and give the impression that you are genuine. And, perhaps most importantly, you must never expose any of the members of the Opossum Clan. That is the code. If you do, you will drown in fake accusations. You will be inundated with fake opportunities. So much fake will be coming at you, you will not know the real world from the fake world. Your fake game will have crumbled and no one will want anything to do with you.

In nature, the possum wraps its tail around a tree branch and hangs upside down in an unfamiliar, contrary position. They have left the main current and turned their life upside down. In the end, they play dead, at least that is how it appears. But you can never tell if they are playing or not.

OTTER

Otters are rather small mammals that project a large presence. They have thick two-layered fur—the thickest in the animal kingdom. Because of that fur several species of otters are endangered. They are intelligent, even brilliant at times. Otters are charming creatures with effervescent energy. They are playful and entertaining. They are both lively and lovable. Unless they are out-and-out enemies, they mix well with other animals.

The otter's pelt is considered a prize by many indigenous peoples. They are considered to have water energy and are used in ceremony. They are often used to make pouches that will hold sacred objects. The spirit of the otter is often called upon during healing practices.

The Otter Clan is a woman's clan. Theirs is a feminine power. The feminine is limitless. It will help you find and live a life for which you are best suited. Call to otter's power to help you laugh, to help you see the humor in most every situation. Ask yourself when you forgot how to have fun. See if you can find the inner child that began to take life too seriously, the one who wanted to play but shut down in a demanding environment. Find that child within yourself and give her candy, bubblegum, or toys—whatever makes her happy. Try to find and commit to her simple joys. Have fun weekends. If you return this joy to your inner child, that aspect of self, it will attract more of the same.

Members of the Otter Clan are friendly and devoted to each other. They flow in the freedom of love. They are without guile and they draw you into their many charms. They have a certain smile, a certain twinkle in their eye. They love to tease and play with any serious notions—not in an offensive way. They invite you to let go of your inhibitions, take a romp on the wild side, and laugh at yourself because you have strayed so far from your natural state. They remind you that simple pleasures are everywhere—if you would but open your mind and grasp them.

Otter Clan people are curious and creative. They teach nonjudgment, openness, and the dynamic of sharing. They have a special place in their heart for children. They are empathetic. They are psychic. They are kind. This is the energy at the core of the Otter Clan.

To discover this clan, find women who are centered, joyful, and inquisitive in a nonthreatening way. Otters are never mean spirited. To them, life is a mixture of fun and games. They are happy and you can move into that place with them. They are in the flow of life. They escort you into their magical world of personal fulfillment, joy, and wonder. Indeed, you may wake up and realize you are at the center of the welcoming Otter Clan.

OWL

The first thing an owl does upon waking is preen and shimmy, stretch and nibble, and comb its feathers with its claws. They have large oval faces. Their eyes are huge, round, and see straight ahead. They have the ability to turn their head over a half circle to change views. Because they can pinpoint sound and have binocular vision, prey doesn't stand a chance. Another edge they have is the ability to fly silently. They can swoop down without their prey knowing what hit them.

Owls were on the earth at the time of the dinosaurs. They are the old ones, the ones who have successfully persisted. Ancient cultures had a wide range of beliefs about the owl. Some thought they were the wisest of birds. Others, however, said they were birds of ill omen, bringing sickness and death or at the very least, a huge, painful transition. Most agree owls are mysterious and possess uncanny gifts.

Owls own the night and know everything that is being done in the darkness. They help women shamans with healing ceremonies. Owls are a conduit for spirit messages. They translate what the spirits are saying, repeating it back in language the shaman can understand. Owls know the silence and the dark. They are sometimes called night eagles.

Owl Clan people turn their head, eyes wide, and stare right through you. Their language can throw you in a panic because it presses your buttons—buttons better left unpressed. Owl's nocturnal hooting, more like a quick succession of witchy vocables, can make one shiver.

Mercifully, these people are usually understated, occasionally turning unexpectedly scary. Their large eyes can stop you cold.

Members of the Owl Clan ask probing questions. It can be alarming, as though they have put the last piece of the puzzle that is you in place and suddenly the big picture is complete. This sudden shattering of ego is a frightening experience, this coming unraveled by the use of a dark language of the night. Such are the disquieting moments when the owl presence is near.

Owl people have acute hearing and listen to what is being said on all levels of conversation. They teach us to listen. There are many sage elders in this clan—elders who know everything there is to know about everything. They see through self-righteousness and pretense. They have no tolerance for hypocrisy. They are keepers of the lost knowledge of antiquity. They are associated with women's mysteries, clairvoyance, wisdom, secrecy, hidden truth, the ability to deceive, shape shifting, and use stealth, witchcraft, and sorcery. Caution, practitioners of these hidden arts may put a spell on you.

Modern-day people in the Owl Clan are usually pagans. They may be people involved with nature religions or various mystery schools. They may be involved in Wicca or Neo-Druidism. They might be people involved in alchemy, past life regression, shamanism, earth mysteries, astrology, kabala, or prophesy. Anyone, in short, seeking their true path that has been occluded from them. If this description fits your inclinations, the hidden Owl Clan may be unveiled for you and beckon you to enter.

PLUMED SERPENT

The Plumed Serpent was once a god—a spirit being that was part bird and part snake swimming in the galactic seas of the heavens. The energy of the Plumed Serpent correlates roughly to the planet Venus. But it is not the Venus of Western astrology. The ancient astronomers of Turtle Island had different beliefs of the morning and evening star. Venus was not so much about love and beauty. It was called the "Great Star." The Venus of the morning caused everyone to stay indoors. It was considered to be bad energy and they did not want to catch the rays of the evil light. The feathered serpent emerged from the deep study of this planet.

The Plumed Serpent's dualistic energy is often linked to pregnancy and the spark of life and Plumed Serpent Clan people live that life to the fullest. They possess a heightened consciousness. They have attained an inner bliss at a cellular level. To them, life is a dance of joy. Plumed Serpent people take risks and savor the outcomes, whatever they may be—good or bad. They are efficient and have leadership qualities. Plumed Serpent Clan people flourish and flow with life and can lead you out of bondage and into freedom.

The Plumed Serpent is a primal energy and represents cosmic life force. A plume, often called a fluffy, will float in the air. When someone tries to hit a fluffy, it wafts away so that a plume becomes a teaching about being light of spirit. No force coming at you can hurt you, a good lesson for our times.

A serpent embodies a perfect balance of male and female energies. It is the raw life-supporting, all-pervading, vital power that gives and animates sentient life. The Plumed Serpent came to earth to instruct people how to use it.

The newborn human is not separated from cosmic understanding. They are at one with the simple truth of being. This information falls from the stars. However, the crown of the head soon closes over and the connection to infinite understanding and purity becomes lessened due to this cranial blockage. The brain is connected to the spine and the spine is an energetic pillar, a column, the divine tree through which life force flows—the so-called "channel that leads to God." Indeed, the energy of the spine has been called "serpent fire" and must be transmuted into spiritual energy.

People in the Plumed Serpent Clan are patiently meditating and waiting for the new light that will enlighten all of humanity instead of just a privileged few. They are waiting for the day that our motherworld will be shifted to a world of tolerance, love, and understanding—truly a heavenly garden. They believe this new world will be coming soon.

The direction toward the Plumed Serpent Clan is toward the Morning Star where you will find a stairway. As you climb, you will learn new things and awaken by degrees, mastering various psychological states. Once you do that, you can climb higher to the pinnacle. There you will find realized sisters and brothers in the Plumed Serpent Clan and join with them.

PORCUPINE

Porcupines are the third largest rodents and can be found in many places across the world. They can live up to twenty-five years or more. Sharp, stabbing quills cover their body. Those quills number in the thousands and protect them from predators. The quills sweep back from the head to a flaring bustle of quills in the rear. It is an imposing array of weaponry.

Porcupines are definitely famous for their ability to skewer an adversary. These barbs or quills are constructed in such a way they leave the body of the porcupine and are easily lodged beneath the skin of a victim. The quill, a kind of modified hair, will bore gradually into the flesh, deeper and deeper with each of the victim's movements. Porcupine quills can even become fatal.

Members of the Porcupine Clan exude a nonchalant confidence and sincerity. They are night folks. When the sun lowers below the horizon, they are out and about. They are like happy children—enthusiastic, idealistic, and honest. They have powerful logic because they are able to reduce complications to their simplest components. As is said, they tell it like it is. They speak the truth and let the chips fall where they may, often causing a maelstrom around them.

Porcupine Clan people don't bother anybody because no one dares bother them. They are the innocent ones with no desire for rewards. Because of their innocence, they have clarity of vision and oracular powers. As often as not, they are accomplished diviners. They have not separated from their basic truth. They trust in the spirits moving them. They are free from fear and take no thought of consequences for their actions. Porcupine people are peacefully independent and seemingly never grow up. They are always content and happy.

Having the porcupine's spiritual essence in your life will give you a sense of well-being and make you happier. It will make you unafraid and vastly creative. The porcupine path is a process of trusting spirit. As you close in on your goal, you will realize the power and protection surrounding you. Trust in karma. Simply know that anyone who actively tries to harm you will be impaled.

Move your attention to the beyond, to your past life connections and lifetimes that have defined you. Remember. Build upon your internal identity. Go back to your true porcupine self. It may be old and bent, but also as gleeful as a happy tot on a busy bouncy playground. Such exuberance is seldom met unless you are a member of the Porcupine Clan. Living peacefully and happily is the best reward.

RABBIT

Rabbits are furry and have fluffy short tails. In the wild, their color varies from tan to brown to brackish gray. Their eyes are large and prominent and their ears are most often very long. They have prehensile front lips used to grasp food. Their hind legs are strong and they are powerful runners. They are intelligent and attentive to their environment, as well they should be—they are the prey of many animals. Perhaps that is also why they are so unbelievably prolific.

Profligate rabbits do have a few laughable and negative qualities. They freeze or take flight when they think they are being threatened. They need to separate being actually in danger from false perceptions and act accordingly. They have a quaint, dignified air. In some instances, they feel vulnerable. But when they feel safe, they have a good time. They romp. They gambol.

Rabbit is a mythic figure the world over. In some stories the rabbit appears as a witch's or a sorcerer's familiar, serving as a companion and helper. A good deal of myth has rabbit down as a con man, a thief, a trickster and swindler, a cruel and hateful creature, cunning and treacherous. Still others suggest rabbits are rash and thoughtless.

In one such story, the rabbit trades his eyes with a blind man in order to have a life of luxury, good food, and sweet water to drink. Unfortunately, without eyes, he trips, breaks things, has many painful accidents, and gets lost in the forest. When the once-blind man returns, he gives the poor rabbit back his eyes saying he has immensely enjoyed seeing again. The blind man and the rabbit happily exchange with each other and return to their former lives. Both have learned lessons and are better for the experience.

The greatest lessons of the rabbit way are how to power through fear, drop defensiveness, and become the loving tender person you truly are. The Rabbit Clan is highly social and participants have enriching light-hearted celebrations, ceremonies, and dances. Many tribes hold the rabbit dance. There are also rabbit powwow dances. Less traditional rabbit dances that have some resemblance to the square dance have also been performed. Ceremonies in Native America are not talked about much, but there are various rabbit ceremonies, many of them done by children. Look no further than Easter for a rabbit celebration that has seeped into much of tribal Native America.

Call on this clan in early springtime when the cold, dark days of winter are over and there is a new freshness in the world. Be open to new comforts and new abundance. Gray days and depression are gone, at least for the time being. The world is blooming; the trees, the flowers, and excitement and promise fill our minds and hearts. Connecting with the Rabbit Clan will fill your life with cheerfulness.

Be quick like a bunny and follow the rabbit as it takes you on a magic journey. The rabbit is a guide to discovering your way. You will feel like you are a rabbit pulled from a magician's hat when you are basking in the affection and love at the center of the Rabbit Clan.

RED WILLOW

Red Willow is sacred and teaches about respect and spirituality. Sweat lodges are built out of this flexible plant. The tree grows near water and prefers damp earth. It is a symbol for balance and longevity. The small tree's long, narrow leaves can be chewed or made into a tea. Aspirin first came from the tree's reddish bark, which produces salicin, an active chemical in aspirin. The bark can also be used for smoking, usually mixed with tobacco.

The smoke of red willow bark gives protection. Like tobacco, red willow can be used as an offering to spirits. It is also used to make purposeful prayer ties to be used in ceremonies. These colorful little medicine bundles hold prayers just as tobacco does. Red willow symbolizes great wisdom and open-mindedness. It is used in the preparation of sacred red paint, but in this instance it is not war paint but peace paint.

Members of the Red Willow Clan are bendable like a willow wand. That being said, they never compromise their principles. You can hold to Red Willow Clan people for comfort and support. Their roots go deep into the earth. You can trust them to be strong and understanding. They are kind. They are introspective. They have a deep empathy and understanding of themselves and others. Their energy is cleansing. They don't judge you. They are respectful and seek to promote spiritual harmony among differing groups.

A sprig of red willow is carried for spiritual defense. Like most spirit clans, silence is a doorway to enter. As mentioned, the red willow is associated with sweat houses or sweat lodges and therefore with water and fire, cleansing and rebirth. Go to the old people of this clan and you will discover much about yourself you didn't know previously. Be like the supple red willow and always spring back.

The clan is said to keep the ancient Red Willow arrow medicine bundle containing four sacred arrows of different colors. Instructions for use of the bundle were received in a sweat lodge vision, hundreds, possibly even thousands of years ago. It is said the red willow shafted arrows are true and straight with hawk feather fletching. The bundle is opened only rarely on very special occasions such as initiating new clan members or for honoring ceremonies. Sometimes it is opened during a clan member's vision quest.

REED

Reed may refer to a harmless enough looking cane or stick but it is, in fact, a deadly weapon when used by an accomplished martial artist. Many martial arts practices include stick fighting. Learning this form of self-protection gives you confidence. It teaches about the weapon's strengths, weaknesses, and limitations. A cane can strike with a punishing force or a deadly force. The use of a stick or cane is an ancient form of combat. Its knowledge can save your life in certain situations.

Members of the Reed Clan carry the cane of empowerment, authority, and justice. They are exacting and follow the principles of unity, fellowship, and brotherly love. They seek to make life happier and ameliorate harmful conditions. Reed Clan people are dignified and protected, the reed or cane being their first weapon. It is the instrument employed by the clan for self-defense and the protection of others. The actual canes may be decorated with insignias of rank and meaning such as beaded strips, animal fur, ribbons, and eagle or other feathers. Some just keep it simple, plain wood with a curved or bulbous handle.

There are any number of variations of the name of the Reed Clan: Pole Clan, Cane Clan, Walkingstick Clan, Staff-In-Hand Clan, Oak Stick Clan, Red Stick Clan, and so on. These clans are all honorable and distinguished. In clan meetings, some Reed Clan members practice fighting techniques. This is no soft martial art. It is a hardcore, devastating martial art if it is used—harsh, assaultive, and unrelenting. Even elders of the clan are formidable practitioners and teach younger members secret martial arts methodology, which becomes spiritual in nature after long practice. Enlightenment, the masters tell you, doesn't come about contemplating your bellybutton or kicking back and becoming complacent. Enlightenment comes about with steel discipline and iron willpower. It is a daunting path but it leads to perfection. In perfection we merge with the infinite and become a Buddha.

Some Reed Clan people have been fabled martial artists. That feeble-looking older person hobbling down the street using a cane may be able to painfully crush just about any enemy, though they would much rather bow out of a fight than easily give an antagonist the sound thrashing they so richly deserve. Members of the Reed Clan hold secret ceremonies, processions, rituals, and dances. They have clan songs and they keep oral history. Bow in to the dojo of the Reed Clan. The Reed Clan path may be long and difficult but in any case you will experience spiritual growth. You will find it to be a temple of the gods who have struggled with themselves to be the best.

If you want to learn how to take care of yourself and keep in good physical condition, consider the Reed Clan. If you pay attention and look in the right places, this clan is easy enough to find. The clan teaches, not only self-defense but also self-assurance, self-confidence, and gender equality. There are many other benefits such as self-discipline and stamina. Martial arts can be deep meditation and can put you in touch with your stillness, your center. If you haven't found this clan, learning Japanese swords is a good practical beginning since the teachings are similar.

In the end Reed Clan members are responsible for keeping the peace.

ROADRUNNER

He runs and he runs, the roadrunner does. He seems incapable of merely walking. He needs to put on the speed. The red-eyed, bushy-headed roadrunner with a streaked body is quick enough to catch a rattlesnake, a most favored food.

The roadrunner is a dark brown and white bird in the cuckoo family, a so-called ground bird. They have long legs and run faster than humans. They can lift off and fly, but only for a few seconds. They are born to run on desert paths and the open roads that give them their name. They have long tail feathers that twitch when they are on the move. The roadrunner is legendary for speed.

Seeing a roadrunner may bring unexpected, abrupt travel plans, say a move to the other side of the world. They often cause cognitive misperceptions and unexplainable occurrences. Did you ever, for instance, stand talking to a person filled with nervous energy, looking here and there? Suddenly they have vanished. No warning. Gone. Just like that with no sighs or goodbyes. That person must have been some speedy individual with the spirit of a roadrunner.

Members of the Roadrunner Clan are the original multitaskers. They may be truck or bus drivers, tour or group leaders. They may be adventurers who cut trails through unknown territory. They are always juggling several things at the same time. Before they can explain what they are doing, they are off on their next venture. They are difficult to pin down. Roadrunners are called by several names including "snake eaters" and "chaparral birds." They are able to take off like a shot often with no particular reason for doing so. They think fast and can easily change directions; some people say roadrunners can shift into other realities.

Roadrunner people are survivors and you will be too if you are admitted into this unusual clan. They are humorous. They always get what they want and they rapidly adapt to every condition. They remain optimistic and free. There is no better ally than roadrunner to help you meet with rapid change and shifting realities.

If you are a speedy person and have little patience with stuck and slow-moving individuals, plus you have the need to zip ahead, chances are you will fit in well with the Road-runner Clan. They are people who no one can follow. They switch directions and their mind surges ahead to where their body immediately catches up. To be in this clan, you have to be fast on every level. A roadrunner can move so fast you expect a sonic boom. This clan is an elusive one, but if you can handle the highest order of physical, mental, and spiritual agility, then by all means you are suited to this clan.

SAGE

Sage is a shrub-like, fragrant plant—a branched perennial—and varieties of it are found all over the world. Smoldering sage in an abalone shell, small iron skillet, bowl, or other container is a balm to the spirit of spirits. Sage smoke calms and rids one of negative vibrations, feelings, and unhealthy attachments.

Sage is burned in many traditional ceremonies and is frequently kept with sacred power objects such as pipes and medicine bundles. Some people make sage bracelets, anklets, or necklaces to wear during ceremonies and other spiritual observances.

Members of the Sage Clan walk the medicine walk, connect with good spirits, and enhance the well-being of others. They are just as the name suggests, sages, meaning profoundly wise. They are related to the plant and their ancient teachings derive from its use. Sage Clan people possess purifying energies.

A story is told that there was once a woman whose husband was taken to a star by star people. He left happily, assuring his wife he was going to a better world. The man entered a strange silver disk followed by several star people. It streaked upward and turned a fiery red. The strange craft disappeared into the night sky leaving only the moonlight and a vast twinkling starscape.

The beautiful woman sobbed and folded onto the ground. Her tears flowed and would not be stanched. She lay on the buffalo grass for a long while, rolling on her back to look once more at the star-filled night sky. Hours later she fell asleep and had a most unusual dream.

In the dream she was sitting by a fire inside a cave. Light from the fire bathed the cave walls in flickering crimson.

Across from the fire was a fearsome, disheveled old white-headed woman—a witch.

"Why are you here?" asked the gnarly old witch in a scratchy voice.

"My husband has been taken away to a star by star people. I will surely die from this separation; I feel so all alone. I feel I must kill myself."

The witch flushed in anger. "Foolish girl, life is a great accomplishment and it is not to be discarded at a whim. I will not let this happen. This is what you must do if you want to quit feeling sorry for yourself and help people. But first you must agree to do it. Is that understood?"

She nodded her head and the witch instructed her.

The woman awoke from the intense dream at twilight. The witch had told her to stand where the silver craft had been where there was a wide circle of burnt vegetation. She stood at its center, facing north. She prayed, and once her prayer was finished, she said the three magic words the witch had taught her to say.

Her entire body suddenly shivered. She felt a pulling weight at her feet. Roots broke through her moccasins going deep into the ground and grayish-green leaves spread over her entire body. The grieving woman became the very first sage plant—a plant used to this day for spiritual purification. The morning sun broke in the heavens and the sunlight shown over her new incarnation.

These are the three magic words she spoke: "I love you." Sage Clan teachings concern wisdom and physical and spiritual protection. The sweet smell of sage smoke is centering and may well lead you to this magnificent spirit clan.

SHELL

A shell refers to the hard outer covering of a marine animal such as a scallop or an oyster. Shells are found on beaches the world over, on both salt and fresh water shores. Shells are empty because the animal has died. What is left is the protective layer created by the sea animal.

There are people who are flesh and blood and live in our three-dimensional world but they have disappeared from it. They have found the great emptiness. They are empty because they are most full. They are at one, in perfect peace, in perfect balance, and they live by their inner and outer light. One must be awake to see them, to understand their emptiness, but one has to be completely awakened to know them and their spirit.

Shell Clan people usually do some ordinary job, possibly related to the arts, like bookbinding, or landscaping. Or they may choose jobs related to water, such as cleaning swimming pools—not much to envy here. Think again. They are not obvious, and yet, they are humble masters of life and all its vicissitudes. They are the unseen teachers of deep spiritual precepts. Accordingly, love is their highest order of business. They are the incarnation of spiritual love. This is the most that can be expected of anyone. There are many kinds of shells but they all have one similar attribute, emptiness. A shell once contained a living being. An empty shell reminds us that life is temporary and this house we live in is temporary. Perhaps in looking at a shell we can remember our original state—our true nature of spirituality. Emptiness comes with the realization of cosmic love.

To experience emptiness, we must have complete non-attachment. This world appears desirable and though it may look solid, it is impermanent. Each and every one, every thing, every sentient being is going to transform. We are all on a journey to the great emptiness. Letting go of all attachments, we become free here and now. There is then nothing to reach for and grasp, nothing to attach to. We can then enjoy this splendid ride called life.

Emptiness is not boredom, loneliness, or depression. It is not grief. It is not existential dread or alienation. In the phenomenal world of change and the world of changing changes, it is the art of letting go—of releasing the banks of the river and flowing happily. The river flows to the ocean and becomes the ocean.

If you can experience cosmic connection while looking at a simple shell, you are near to your clan. Have an open heart to receive the wisdom teachings of the shell. There are gifts hidden inside of you, waiting for you to discover them. And when we are empty, we are full.

SNAKE

Snakes are limbless reptiles. They can be tiny or up to twenty-five or more feet in length. They move rapidly, thrusting forward in a repeating motion. They glide noiselessly, gliding hither, thither, and yon. They come in different lengths and colors. Some are poisonous and some are not. Snakes have long, black, forked tongues, which act as feelers, darting out and examining the environment.

Snakes are cold-blooded and hibernate. Hibernation connects them with dream and visioning states. A snake exists in the form of a line. It can bite its own tail and become circular with no beginning or end—a symbol of infinity. Snakes are also one of the earliest symbols for wisdom. Beware of the warning rattle. The diamonds. Other snakes come. Ringed in black and scarlet. The tie snakes, the whip snakes, they come. The racers, the garters, and the orange ones, the bull snakes come. And the pythons, the cobras come. These are some of the oldest healing clans on earth.

Never speak ill of snakes except in the winter when they are hibernating and can't hear you. Never kill one. Instead, ask the snake spirit to transmute the pain and suffering in this world.

Snake Clan people are imbued with primal life force. The rattlesnake is the over-chief of all the snake clans. According to oral history, the rattlesnake was once a man. He chose to become a snake. He fell to the ground and rolled over and over, twisting in anguish. His limbs sunk into his body. He elongated and grew a long tail. He grew scales. They covered his neck and his head was swallowed and became a snake's head.

The various snake clans were put on earth to save us from extinction. They hold a key to the earth's survival. Snake Clan energy brings inevitable change and bears a closeness to the very sources of life. Snake Clan people are keepers of lost knowledge. They hold wisdom dating from long before human history. They are the great shamans, doctors, and medicine people. If healing yourself or others is your passion, call to the snakewoman or snakeman for help. Let the snake be your guide to a spiritual and physical rebirth.

Members of the Snake Clan have a most balanced energy. They are charming (no pun intended), even in their interactions with others. They have enigmatic healing capabilities and they may make their living from a remedial profession. Their unblinking gaze is electric, chilling. It is as though they lock you in it and then probe deeply into your safe and secure self, that self with no admittance. Yet the overly intense serpent slithers all through your naked psyche. Snakes tell you to transmute your poisons and transform your mental energies and become wise like a serpent. Perhaps you will shed your skin and have a rebirth and a reinvention. It is a calling to join with a Snake Clan, one of the highest energetic forces here on earth.

SNIPE

Snipe birds are close relations to sandpipers. They are wading birds frequently found among reeds. They have long bills which they use to catch elusive worms, snails, and other treats. They are rather plump. When snipe birds are flushed in the wild, they escape by running in a zigzag pattern leaving as little a target as possible. They move. They dart. They make confusing twists and turns. They quickly disappear from view. If you lose sight of them, you might as well not try to find them afterward because you can't. They're gone.

The mother snipe builds her slightly sunken nest on a simple bed of leaves and grass and sometimes covers it over with grass tufts. Eggs are usually four in number, and olive in color with brown speckles. If the mother snipe feels threatened in any way, she packs up the eggs or chicks and leaves for safer ground.

In New Zealand the night call of the snipe is said to send chills down the spine of tribal peoples and the birds are greatly feared as harbingers of evil. They are said to have the power of invisibility, the power to disappear from view.

Members of the Snipe Clan are martial in appearance, with a straight back and, as often as not, are rather ridged looking. They are in fact members of a warrior clan. One can easily imagine them leading a pipe and drum marching band. The Snipe Clan is an airy, intelligent group and the snipe bird is their guiding spirit. They are caretakers of the earth and have an affinity with water. They meet often near a river or marsh and have intricate ceremonies. They are keepers of the sacred medicine waters and often run sweat lodges.

Snipe Clan people are masters of camouflage and, in warfare, ambush—hence the word "sniper." Snipers can be a long way off drawing a bead on a target. They take aim at an enemy and kill it. They never get comfortable in one place and quickly move to another. Sniping takes patience, concentration, and mental strength.

Snipe people often live on a shoreline or near a lagoon. Rivers or lakes will do in a pinch. The Snipe Clan is elusive to some but blatantly apparent to others. They might be football or basketball coaches. They might be police officers or private detectives. They might be in a marching band. They can be high-ranking military personnel. Some are martial artists. Snipe bird form, known as kata, is taught in various martial arts, including aikido, karate, and jujutsu.

The Snipe Clan teaches self-knowledge and working with intent. If it is your intent to find this clan, you will. So set your intention if this clan appeals to you. The snipe digs for information and so must you. The Snipe Clan may turn up in the most unexpected of places but it will always be near water, the source of life.

SNOW

Snow has covered much of the world at one time or another. It blankets the earth in winter, reflecting most of the sun's energy back into the sky, which is very important to our climate system. When it melts away, it helps fill lakes, rivers, and reservoirs. Snow may seem commonplace, but actually it is a miracle that falls from heaven.

A snowflake is considered to be a spirit being coming to rest upon the earth. Each snowflake is unique, just as all creatures are unique. Floating from above, each flake speaks in its soft angelic voice of silence—a long winter's chant of beauty. The snowflake has faith and knows it will have to let go in form and merge into a new flow of experience.

Similarly, the Snow Clan teaches of letting go into the great silence where there is no "I." For them, "I" is an illusion dripping away. So soon we melt into the oneness. "See me and remember," the snow whispers. "Let go and hold to nothing." Snow Clan people are highly intelligent and are able to flow with change. They are tolerant and nonjudgmental. They have a spiritual bent that is magic.

In an old tale it is told that the earth was once terribly hot, unbearably hot—an uninviting, unlivable place. The sun was burning and wrinkling the people's skin and there was never a minute of relief from the scorching heat.

A noble chief named Yellow Shield called all the people together. There were exhausted, burned-out people as far as the eye could see. The chief held up his arms to the fiery sky. He prayed for a miracle to save his people. As he prayed, thousands of huge white birds suddenly appeared and flew in unfamiliar patterns, around and around above the gathering. They were in a frenzy. The dizzying sight was overwhelming and gave a cooling respite from the punishing heat.

As the chief continued to pray, the birds flew away to the north. The sky turned gray by degrees. A cold wind whipped up. For the first time ever a blizzardy snow began to fall. The people were overjoyed and rubbed themselves with this strange new substance. As the snow fell, it brought beauty and the people realized it was a spiritual gift. The people were evermore grateful. From these happy people a new clan was formed, the Snow Clan.

In a single snowflake abides the spirit of winter, a time to stay warm and move gently onward, a time to consider the wisdom of the elders, a time to use the intellect for problem solving. It is a time for finishing projects, for organizing, a time to detach from self-limiting ideas and behaviors. Winter is a time to find a warmth, a clarity of vision, in short, the knowledge kept by the Snow Clan.

With snow, there is a gift, a purity in the air, a calming feeling. We hear the silence, the voice of Creation. We know the stillness and a time of magic. This is a precious gift indeed, this special time of winter. Put your heart and mind into sharing this miraculous time with others. The season's spirits will lead you to the warm and hospitable Snow Clan.

SPIDER

Spiders have eight legs attached to the fore parts of their body and no antennae. They do not undergo metamorphoses like that of most insects, which means they don't change form. There are many kinds of spiders including trapdoor spiders and water spiders, but here we are concerned with the spiders that spin those remarkable webs. The webs are traps to catch prey on which the spider feeds.

Spider teaches that we humans have a web. We are at the web's center and strands of this web ray off in every direction. We can meditate each morning and see what is caught in our personal web and we can either keep it or get rid of it. We will want to keep our webs symmetrical, free of impediments, and strong.

Let the spider spin you—that is to say, bring you good fortune. Spider Clan people acknowledge a great creatrix mother, Spider Mother the Mistress of Nets, and the fundamental unity at the center of the multiverse. From her, the women learned weaving. She wove the web of life and flung a dew-laden web into the empty sky where the dewdrops became the stars. The clan believes she is the source of sacred language. She wove the alphabet into her celestial web. Each letter is a doorway into other worlds. She taught the women how to make a web to catch dreams. These dream and spirit catchers are used in ceremony as the entering points for good spirits.

She is sometimes called Old Spider Woman. She gave the children string games for their amusement. In this game, a figure or design is made by manipulating string. The game can be played by one or several people who use their fingers, wrists, feet, and even their mouth. The act may or may not include storytelling as the figure is being created.

She taught people how to weave bands of energy for personal protection. This is a method for psychic self-protection used by women to shield themselves and their children from negative energies. Prayers are said and imagined woven light is projected guarding each concerned person. Imagining, some say, is our consensus reality anyway.

In an old story, Spider Woman, who is also called Sneakup Woman, steals fire and then offers it to various animals to use. They are afraid of it and all refuse the gift. She finally offers fire to humans, who quickly realize its value and take it. Soon they have heat and warmth, cooking abilities, and firelight. Old Spider Woman's gifts to the people are many—fire, games, colorful weavings, and some say even the gift of life.

People in the Spider Clan are weavers, chanters, and enchanters. They have patience and they always have a few tricks up their sleeve. They have a long oral tradition and are wonderful poets and story tellers. They have extended, lovely chants that connect you with a deep and essential mind stream. Spiders appearing in visions or dreams are power symbols. Good luck is coming. This clan initiates you in the use of catching medicine to use for capturing any desire you might have. With Spider Clan power you can weave your own comforting world.

SPRUCE

Elders taught that spruce trees hold up the sky and their spirit guards the north direction. An evergreen tree of many varieties, spruce grows in northern forests and can reach as much as three-hundred-feet tall. Their shape is conical and they have whorled branches with needlelike leaves. These needles boiled in water make a tea that is high in Vitamin C. Sucking on the gummy resin from an injured spruce will lessen thirst.

Once upon a time there was a powerful medicine man called Puma and he had many wives and children. He was a wonderworker. He could transform himself into other beings. He could bend reality any way he wanted it. He healed many people from terrible illnesses. All the people owed him a debt of gratitude for some marvelous miracle he had performed.

Puma became obsessed with the one woman in his village who was not the least interested in him. Her name was Fawn. The more he sought her, the colder and more indifferent she acted toward him. She was immune to his love medicines.

One day, Puma decided to secretly follow Fawn when she left the village as she did early each morning. About a mile away from the village at a higher elevation, there stood a stately spruce tree. She spread out a blanket on the ground and sat beneath the tree and appeared to be meditating on the beautiful evergreen.

Puma watched her for several days. Finally he approached her. Her dress was beautiful with masterful bead and quill-work. Her moccasins were also covered in the finest bead-work. Her lustrous long dark hair was braided. She smelled of smoke, of dusky woodlands, of mysterious scents—a perfume of yearning.

Fawn became aware of his presence and opened her eyes, which had been tightly shut. She flinched at seeing him.

"Oh, I didn't mean to startle you," said Puma. "I couldn't help but wonder what you are doing here under this tree."

"This tree is my husband," Fawn said. "Each day my husband speaks to me and gives me instructions of how to serve him. I have pledged myself and I find all the joy and happiness one can imagine here. This spruce tree, my husband, fills me with love and I can love no other."

"What are you saying, woman? The mystery created women to be with a man, a man like me, not a tree. You need to be with me in the way our creator intended."

Fawn turned her face from Puma. "Please be gone," she said. "And never disturb me when I am with my husband. Never speak to me again. I will never again speak to you or have anything more to do with you."

The next morning Puma used his magical changing powers to go inside the spruce tree. He watched Fawn come and spread her blanket and sit in front of him. He watched her all day until she left but something terrible had happened. He couldn't get out of the spruce tree, try as he might. He has been locked inside since that day. Now the spruce tree has the medicine man's powers.

Over the years the medicine man in the tree has exchanged marriage vows with many thousands of beautiful women. He is always filled with longing because he cannot consummate his vows. Men sometimes carry a ball of spruce pitch in the hopes that the spruce brides will mistake them for their husbands and lavish them with their favors. Spruce wood carries vital forces and is used as a helper bringing good luck and blessings. Carrying a small branch of spruce is soothing and has rejuvenating qualities.

Spruce Clan people are constant. Trees and wizardry go together. Spend time with a spruce tree. Make a commitment to the Spruce Clan, the solid people who are said to hold up the world and have miraculous powers. Be observant. Listen with your deepest self. Become a modern-day spruce wizard by following the intuitive wisdom that leads you to the Spruce Clan.

SQUASH

The squash plant is one of the Three Sisters: corn, beans, and squash—plants that were planted together by Native American farmers. Squash was, and still is, a staple food. The blossom is dipped in egg and fried. The squash itself, and the seeds, are also eaten. Aside from being a food crop, squash can be dried and used as dance rattles. Today, these rattles are used by many tribes.

You will perhaps recognize the squash blossom, the two twisted coils of hair in the hairstyles of women in the paintings of artist R. C. Gorman and other noted Native American painters. It is the traditional hairstyle of unmarried women. The trumpet-looking squash blossoms were considered guardians of the land and the people. They are used decoratively and also represent clouds and the blessing that is rain. Squash blossoms spilled on the ground during ceremony symbolizes the renewal of all human and animal life. The act is a plea that the cycles in nature support growth, fertility, and new beginnings. There are many traditional blossom dances on Turtle Island during the course of the changing seasons.

Squash are one of the earliest known food plants. Squash blossom petroglyphs can be found in the mountains of Arizona and archeologists have uncovered ancient containers in Mexico containing squash seeds from before 7000 BC. Interestingly, seeds were ground up and mixed with cornmeal to make a good tasting, nutritious bread.

Plants are more than a good salad. All plants have magical qualities. Science now knows that plants are sentient beings. Plants have always been thought to be so by indigenous peoples. Plants have intelligence and great sensitivity and respond to love and respect. The have photoreceptors and are aware of any presence near them. Scientists today also say that plants do mathematics and are even kind to other plants. Plants can communicate with animals and various other types of vegetation by releasing a range of compounds and pleasing smells.

Squash Clan members stress growth, are open, and embrace all people. They are practical. Both men and women of the clan are honest and direct. They are peaceful and tolerant. They are serious but not too serious. They are charitable, kindhearted, and trustworthy. They love the earth. They love gardening and do what they can to protect the environment. Their clan has unity, love, and devotion. Men are from the sky—spiritual. Women are of the earth—substance. Men don't give spiritual advice in this clan; only Clan Mothers and women can because it is felt that the laws of spirit are different on the ground.

People of the Squash Clan are married to plants in a certain way through ritual and ceremony. They view plants as their relations and communicate to them through their heart. So if you feel you are connected to the plant spirits and the divas of leaf and flower, you will assuredly find your way to this clan.

SQUIRREL

Squirrels are bushy-tailed rodents with large eyes and rest-less energy. They have much expression in their tails. Most are arboreal and have strong hind legs. Squirrels can be various colors but are mostly orange. They have four front teeth that grow continuously throughout their life. Their diet is mostly nuts and seeds.

Squirrels are found all over the planet. There are hundreds of species—tree squirrels, ground squirrels, and flying squirrels. The last are endangered. Squirrels are shy and make their homes in tree holes or build a nest similar to birds. They don't like to be in anyone's line of vision. They are excellent climbers, driven to reach the treetops. They always find a hidden place to avoid danger. Dreams about traveling the tree trails often denote a kinship with squirrels.

Squirrels have differing habitats and differing ways of living. Essentially, however, they synchronize with life's demands and are prepared for most eventualities. They have had the foresight to store things away for a later date. Squirrels don't mind stirring up trouble. They may have strong premonitions of impending disasters. They are sometimes tipsters who tell people to prepare by storing items that might be needed in a time of crisis. They give advice and information about how to best shield from a worst-case scenario

Squirrel Clan people usually have a lot of nervous energy and like to chat and chatter with others. They don't mind throwing in a little titillating gossip now and then. The clan is successful and prosperous. Members are resourceful. They think about and prepare for the future. Chances are good when you meet them they will have out their day planner to jot down notes for some upcoming event or obligation. Like the squirrel, they can be mesmerizing and exude great charm. They are thrifty, gregarious, and have the ability to solve difficult problems. They always have a trove of goodies secreted away, and a hefty bank account along with an envious stock portfolio. They probably have a stash or two hidden away waiting for a rainy day. They also have an obligation to protect forests.

Squirrel Clan meetings are boisterous, noisy affairs. The Squirrel clan has the responsibility to perform the necessary rituals associated with both solar and lunar eclipses and for other heavenly phenomenon such as meteor showers. This duty falls heavily upon the Black Squirrel Clan.

Call on this clan in times of upheaval and trouble. They are hard workers. They not only save things, but they also save lives. They can show you what to let go of and what to keep. They will also teach you how to acquire new gifts and skills that can move you along in life's process. Go ahead, go out on a limb. Learn to be balanced and you will find many new potential gifts on each branch. You may even find impressive philosophical and intellectual gifts from this clan.

SUN

The sun is the most powerful source of energy—of light and heat. A metaphysical sun lights our consciousness. The significance of our bright physical sun, our star, is the light it shines on our planet to sustain life. It is symbolically related to the right hand. Our days and nights are defined by whether the sun is above or below the horizon. We are all in a symbiotic relationship with this solar energy. We must have light and since we must, the sun is the most important of heavenly bodies. In most cultures the sun is a symbol for absolute authority and it must be noted that the sun can burn, kill, and destroy. Still, it is the sun that illuminates our spiritual minds and protects us from false teachers that teach darkness.

Sun Clan people are celestial warriors, intent on spiritual victory. Female or male, they are centered just as the sun is the center of our planetary system. Sun clans and clan members are plentiful on all continents. As a rule, they teach happiness and positive thinking and display an aura of nobility. They are straight ahead and energetic. They open the golden door to treasure. They are creative and generous to a fault. The sun provides warmth and light, as do members of this clan. They are well off, have good finances, exceptional personal power, and magnetism. They are strong willed and their desires typically hold sway.

Members of this clan walk with the energy of the sun, the life-giver. The sun has a male warrior essence, and gives an awareness of protection and a helpful solar relationship. The sun symbolizes reasoning, justice, and logical consistency. It is associated with stability, growth, happiness, reason, and peace. A fiery sun also symbolizes passion.

Sun Clan people hold the light and the center. They provide a much-needed positive energy—the kind of energy that makes progress possible, be it in agriculture, economics, or personal development. They furnish a true support for abundance and prosperity.

Sun dances have been danced on Turtle Island for millennium. The dancers acknowledge the life-giving sun and pray that life can continue. They pray for our mother planet, a sustainable environment, and the well-being of all the animals and all peoples—that we may all have good and satisfying lives. The sundance is the great dance of renewal.

If you are drawn inside yourself to your inner sun and feel a connection to the outer sun, it is the first level of initiation. You may soon find yourself in the brightest of clans bathed in golden light of your spiritual sun realization. And you will find yourself in league with the beating solar heart of all worlds.

TADPOLE

A tadpole's early life is spent in water. Jellylike masses of transparent goo dotted with tiny black spots can be seen floating near the shore. Each of these black spots is a frog's egg. Little by little the tadpole gains strength enough to break through the egg. From there, they are launched into the dangerous waters of their beginnings. From there it will take them six to nine weeks to transform fully into a frog.

Tadpoles are the underwater people, a symbol for the initiation and emergence into life and its processes. They have a bond with all of life. Like water, they are humble. Water is their home and therefore they are emotive. As is said, they will cry over spilled milk. Like water beats on the shore, they are here to remind us constantly of the beginnings and promises of life. They always urge purification and renewal. The Tadpole Clan celebrates life and purity of spirit. They tell you not to dip your foot into the water but to take the plunge.

There are many stories of tadpoles who take on human form. They become lovers, soldiers, candlestick makers—any person they want to become to participate in the drama of human life. In one such story a tadpole becomes a young man who was smitten by a beautiful girl. She was sought after by every male who laid eyes on her. The newly arrived young man felt he didn't have a chance with her but as soon as she saw him, it was love at first sight. They spent a wonderful night together, holding and comforting each other. Being honest, he told her he was a tadpole who was visiting the human world. He told her to be brave and to face life only on her own terms. He promised to never forget her and that he would always be near her in spirit. When she woke up in the morning, the beautiful young man was gone but the woman had known true love.

Members of the Tadpole Clan continually inspire people to trust their own vision and live up to their highest ideals. They are receptive, introspective, and sensitive. They stress growth—physically, mentally, and spiritually. They are close to the source of life—water. It is their element. Their clan embodies the waters of transformation with messages of wisdom, enlightenment, and co-communications with the elemental world. They have a job to do and they are unconcerned about the future.

Tadpole Clan people are guardians of change and in these lively times, change we must. But don't worry, tadpole teachings bring confidence and self-assurance. We are taking the first ceremonial steps before a great leap and a change of form and consciousness. Water is the basis of all life. It is the first mirror. In precious water all things are cleansed. It is a releasing of the old and a welcoming of the new. We crawl upon the shores of a great ocean to acknowledge the next step of our evolution.

When you feel like you are about to break open, it may be the Tadpole Clan calling you. Tadpole is the spirit of growth and change—a membrane in the dimensions to push against. Your soulmates are close. What you are swimming toward is swimming toward you in the sea of mystery. The Tadpole Clan teaches a beneficent power that emanates from within. Once learned, the way to your clan has been cleared for you.

THUNDER

Lightning causes thunder. It opens a channel in the air and once the lightning is gone, the air collapses back and the sound of thunder is heard. When you see a flash of lightning, you can count the seconds until you hear the thunder. Sound travels much slower than light. The quicker you hear the thunder, the closer the lightning is to you. A lightning strike releases such a big charge of electricity it is several times hotter than the surface of the sun.

Thunder is said to have healed people all over the world, some with incurable illnesses. The wood of trees struck by lightning is a much-treasured article used by shamans and medicine people in various ways. Splinters of it are burned and people bathe in the smoke, which is said to give one the power of the thunderbolt. They become a force to be reckoned with. A powder of the bark of a lightning-struck tree is put in the water when seeds are soaked before planting. This ensures a good crop.

Thunder Clan people are unknowable. They are channels for life force. They are said to have potent creative energies, instant knowledge, and the ability to manifest. At the center of their teachings is the supernatural thunderer. These people have made friends with lightning. They relish it—the flash, the boom, the staggered reports.

In long ago olden times, during the age of myths, there were many beliefs concerning lightning and thunder. Some believed there was a giant red man towering up over the earth who caused thunder and the accompanying cracks of lightning. Others thought there was an enormous bird with loud beating wings causing it.

Members of the Thunder Clan believe that Grandfather Thunder is their relative. They believe their grandfather washes the earth and keeps it clean. The clan mother who is the last person to enter the lodge during thunder ceremonies sits in the west. At this annual clan meeting, tobacco is burned and they smoke rolled cornhusk and tobacco medicine cigarettes. They give thanks to First Chief, Grandfather Thunder. They pray. They sing. Almost always during this ceremony, thunder is heard along with accompanying crimson lightning flashes.

Thunder Clan people are mercurial. They move at the speed of light and sudden light is their element. They also possess a spiritual light, a metaphor in most religions for the good. It is the business of people in this clan to project a blinding spiritual light, a light that abides only truth. Call on the spirit of thunder before the rain when there is electricity in the air.

TOBACCO

Known as flowering tobacco, the tobacco plant's colorful tubular flowers perfume the air and the hummingbird is credited with its discovery. Among the seventy or more species of tobacco, *Nicotiana tabacum* is the chief source of commercial tobacco. It is a perennial plant grown for its rounded leaves.

Tobacco's true teachings are needed more today than ever. It is a shamanic tool that protects from evil. It is used to fumigate objects and people, cleansing them, sealing them off from harm, and shielding them from attack and imbalance. The smoke is blown and fanned over sick people and gives spiritual strength. Tobacco juice is often spit in the eyes of shamans to give them second sight, the ability to see the future and distant events, and obtain other information. When a shaman blows tobacco smoke—"the visible breath"—upon a person, it imparts magical powers.

Tobacco is a most sacred way and it has been smoked on Turtle Island for untold thousands of years and used in ceremony in every part of the world. There are many myths about the origin of tobacco. Tobacco reminds us that when we take something, we must give something back. When we find a feather, as an example, or a beautiful stone, or see a splendorous rainbow or a majestic eagle, four pinches of dried tobacco, symbolizing the four directions, can be used to show gratitude. It is a gift given back for what has been received. When we have profited greatly, give four pinches of tobacco and say a prayer of thankfulness. In our own life we must give back to the all one day, to the one, to the mystery.

Members of the Tobacco Clan are responsible for gathering, treating, and distributing sacred tobacco to be used in pipe ceremonies and other rituals. Tobacco is the most important Native American plant, a special gift from Creator. It is used as a spiritual offering and as an adjunct to prayer, also as a mediator between the human world and the spirit world.

Generally speaking, men do the planting and women do the harvesting and curing of sacred tobacco. It is used by both men and women as an offering to good spirits for guidance, protection, paying respects, healing, and for expressing gratitude. The plant unifies humans with their animal brothers and sisters, with plant spirits, with the spirits of all of nature—mountains, the land, lakes, oceans, the sky—and ultimately the cosmos itself.

Tobacco Clan people are modest and always live in a sacred manner. They are awakened visionaries with a close personal relationship with creation. Sacred tobacco is a medicine of the complete human, the body, mind, and spirit. It is the great unifier. If this is your clan, you are many times blessed. Traditional use of tobacco has lessened but tobacco clans are mighty. Perhaps the old ways of using tobacco will soon return and the sacred plant will no longer be abused in such disrespectful ways.

Follow the hummingbird to the flowering tobacco plant, at least in spirit. Begin your day with prayers and an offering of sacred tobacco. Tobacco is a gift. Mystery gave sacred tobacco to the humans to bring peace, harmony, and tranquility among them. To find the Tobacco Clan, be centered, realize the spirits, and ask them to lead you to your clan.

TURKEY

Wild turkeys are large, heavy birds and can weigh nearly forty pounds. They sleep roosting on branches high in trees with their flock where no predators, such as coyotes, raccoons, and foxes, can get to them. They can fly up to fifty miles an hour—a fast clip. Male birds will do the turkey strut to attract a mate while emitting distinctive gobbling songs.

Turkeys were first domesticated in southern Mexico around two thousand years ago. They were associated with corn magic and fecundity. Aztecs kept them as pets and for divination purposes. There was a deep empathy between the turkey diviner and the turkey. The diviner was able to observe the behavior of the bird for the most basic bits of information. Moreover, the turkey would often appear in the dreams of the diviner where they could speak a common language. The turkey would tell the diviner of future events and be able to answer the most confounding of questions.

Turkey divination can also take place in formal rituals. Turkey Clan diviners are known for their powers of prophecy through the use of sacred tobacco smoke blown over kernels of sacred seed corn and fanned with a turkey feather fan. By studying the smoke, the diviner is often able to see the shape of coming events.

Turkeys were held as sacred birds and could do as they pleased with no interference. By the time Europeans arrived on the shores of Turtle Island, the turkey had become an important food source. Turkeys were also raised for their feathers, which were used in healing sessions and ceremonies as well as for headdresses and to adorn clothing and blankets.

Turkey Clan people are generous, pure of spirit, and exhibit a loving comprehension of the needs of others. They assist others in attaining a good balance in the give and take of life and have a high degree of sensitivity to the world around them. They are close to the earth. They bless and care for each other and share their gifts.

To members of the Turkey Clan, all of life is a gift and a mystery. You don't have to be a sage or saint to be initiated into a Turkey Clan but it wouldn't hurt. In any case, members of this clan are exceptionally devoted and spiritual people and they give the utmost of themselves in service.

Traditional turkey dances begin in the afternoon and end at dusk. In some of these ancient dances, only the women dance, wearing striking and colorful costumes, and imitating turkey movements. Men drum and sing old tribal songs. Toward the end, men join in the dance if they are selected by a woman. There are similar turkey celebrations throughout Native America.

Turkeys remind us that life is a sequence of give and take and to note where we are in the cycle. To Turkey Clan people, life is a giveaway. They share their gifts. Ultimately, they know that all gifts come from Mystery. If you care for others, give without expectations, and are open, let the Turkey Clan embrace you. But these loving people must learn to remember to give to themselves as well as others.

TURQUOISE

Turquoise means Turkish stone. Both the Turks and the Aztecs mined the aqua blue to green stone many thousands of years ago. The Aztecs mined turquoise near an area known today as Santa Fe, New Mexico. They believed turquoise was related to fire and the sun. The warrior sun was armed with a great turquoise snake. Early each morning the snake would drive the moon and stars from the night sky. The priest of a New Mexico pueblo was called the Priest of the Northern Rains. He kept a large turquoise heart on a special altar. The turquoise heart was known as the Secret Heart of the World.

Turquoise is a very sensitive stone. It unites earth and sky. It is quick to take on the characteristics of its owner, good as well as not so good. Turquoise is one of the oldest talismans—it is said to give good luck and protection from harm. It will lose its luster before a storm. Allegedly, a large turquoise stone in the north of Turtle Island protected the people. It accurately told of approaching danger by turning a darkish gray. Psychics will carry turquoise to enhance their clairvoyance. Legend has it that turquoise stones are the tears of Our Lady of the Skies. She cried when she saw the overwhelming beauty of earth and her tears became turquoise nuggets.

Historically, turquoise may be the oldest of the highly valued stones. Turquoise beads dating back over seven thousand years have been discovered in Iraq. Turquoise had the reputation of giving safety to the owner. Carry some to protect yourself from personal danger and for an uptick in vitality. It was a talisman for kings and emperors.

Rulers of ancient Egypt wore turquoise. For this reason, it was soon coveted by lesser-ranked people. It was acquired by warriors and explorers, and others who were in dangerous occupations. The stone also enhanced the power of medicine people and other healers.

Turquoise Clan people are well to do and rarely sad. When they initiate a project, they see it through to the end. Many in this clan are accomplished diviners. Turquoise connects clan members to powerful nature spirits. Turquoise Clan teachings include transcendent wisdom—a wisdom beyond knowledge. They teach beauty and peace, which are said to walk hand in hand. They teach respect. If you wish to be respected, be respectful. They teach us to be unpretentious, brave, and honest, and to keep a positive outlook.

Members of the Turquoise Clan carry turquoise, called the "tranquility stone," as a symbol of wisdom, personal power, prosperity, good luck, and for its healing medicine qualities. The clan teaches that the sacred turquoise stone is an intermediary with the spirits of the upper world. The stone will bring high-minded principles down to earth and insist on integrity. If the sky is calling your name, the Turquoise Clan may be your spirit clan.

TURTLE

Turtles are the shy ones, the reticent ones. Turtles are slow moving, egg-laying reptiles, with a protective shell covering them on top and bottom. They live in the salty seas and freshwater lakes and rivers. There are land turtles as well. They come in all sizes from about the size of a silver dollar to gigantic, weighing over a thousand pounds. They are different from all other reptiles. The female turtle can deposit as many as a hundred eggs or as few as one or two.

Turtles live on every continent and have been around since the time of dinosaurs. In myth, a great turtle rose up from the depths of the primeval ocean to create Turtle Island, the North American continent. She brought forth stability to all creatures great and small. Turtles are said to be mediators between the upper and lower world.

Turtle Clan people will protect us from disaster and suffering. They are solid and resolute. They are born grownups. The walk of the turtle and the way of the turtle correspond to ancient cosmic wisdom. They are a microcosm of the universe, of base earth, and the dome of the heavens. As such, they are aware of the highest truths and principles. They persist under the most difficult of circumstances. They know they are walking on the back of a relative, a turtle— Turtle Island. They appear to be slow and easy-going but they continually accomplish their goals.

Members of this clan always feel at home and at peace wherever they are. They have the ability to keep grounded in any situation. They can readily withdraw into themselves and shut out unwanted annoyances. The Turtle Clan teaches that to know heaven we must first know the earth.

They are environmentally aware and do their best to protect the land and the water. They hold ancient knowledge concerning longevity and good health. The spirit of turtle was often called in ceremony. A live turtle was then rubbed over the feet, ankles, and calves to add strength to the legs of ball players, pole climbers, and other people who needed strong legs.

To celebrate and acknowledge the spirit of the turtle on Turtle Island, traditional turtle dances are held by many tribes each year.

Look upon the beauty and bounty of creation. We can thank the Turtle Mother for all that has been provided from her work. If you know yourself to be of the earth, ask the earth spirits to guide you to the Turtle Clan. The turtle guards the health of your spirit. If you meditate on our mother planet and follow your inner guides, you will be led to the Turtle Clan.

WATER

What air is to humans, water is to earth.

Water has the power to cleanse, the power to reflect, the power of regeneration, and truly, water blesses us all. Water makes the corn stand up and after spring rains the wet earth is ready to plant again. The world puts on green robes and is made beautiful because of water. Water has a ripple effect—what you send out will come back to you.

Water Clan people are fluid and have happy, sparkling dispositions. They blossom after rainstorms and appear to be filled with a new life force. They congregate at natural springs, swimming spots, and at beaches. In the early morning hours they can be found near where water spirits dance in sprays along rushing rivers or other coursing waterways.

There are powerful rituals that will make rain. Soon after women wash their hair outdoors, rain will fall. Rainmakers blow their misty breath in each direction and awaken the thunder beings.

Water they say is lowly, humble, seeking always to be the lowest. Water is taken for granted by most people. Not so with traditional indigenous people. Shamans periodically bless the water, first with a series of prayers. They smoke and call for the animal and ancestor spirits to be with them. They acknowledge the spirits of place, the elements, and so on. In some ceremonies they are accompanied by the drumming of water drums, with their curious elastic sounds. They bless each person with a water fowl fan dipped in water and everyone pays respects to the water and recognizes it as essential to their life.

It is the water way to give thanks to all the waters, the deep seas, and the oceans. They thank the creatures in and near water. They are close to the cosmic oceans and are known stargazers and prognosticators. They sense the waters of destiny and the shifts and movements of our times.

Members of the Water Clan have a great responsibility during our current environmental crisis. They are responsible for maintaining all manner of water ceremonies. Yes, water is of primary importance to life, but this clan exists to quench spiritual thirst as well. Water people have good memories, near photographic recall, and can perfectly remember conversations held in years past. They will bring up things about you that you have long since forgotten.

This clan knows prayers to catch fish. They know how to call water babies, the spirits of water, who will frolic nearby and whisper answers to baffling questions. Water Clan people will teach you these water mysteries but you must first give a present they accept, such as tobacco or shiny silver coins. To enter this clan is easy but the work is difficult—keeping water pure and drinkable.

WATER BUG

Water bugs make their home in the muddy bottoms of lakes and rivers. They live in ponds and near waterfalls and neglected pools.

Raven was once lonely and water was silent. Raven made the water bug to skim along the water's surface and frolic and dive down deep so he could watch the activities of the water bug and no longer be lonely.

Members of the Water Bug Clan are in control of their emotions. They are strong and resilient and are said to be shapeshifters. They oftentimes live on boats or houseboats or in houses near water. They have the ability to go deep, and know many powers to transform and use water to enhance mystical discovery. They bring change and also desire, the desire for a regeneration of spirit. They sometimes try to minimize themselves in order to keep from being noticed.

Legend has it that once there was a beautiful woman who Rabbit Man spied but she was a long way off in the distance. He leapt to it and ran so fast that he came to a halt just in front of her, blocking her way. Rabbit Man was right. She had all the right curves and moves and her sweet smile excited him to no end. He was sorely smitten.

Rabbit Man said, "I see a lake but nothing else. Where do you think you are going?"

"I am going home," the woman said.

"But where is home?" asked Rabbit Man.

"I live in the deep down, deep insides of the lake," she answered.

"You are so good I wanted to get together and spend some time together."

"Sit down here by the water's edge and I will send my sisters up from the deep to meet you," said the woman. "My sisters are much better looking than me and I have to be getting along." She pushed him aside.

"Wait," Rabbit Man said.

But the woman had left the shore and was wading deeper and deeper into the water until she turned into a water bug. She then dived down and disappeared into the watery depths.

Rabbit Man was frustrated but sat down as the woman had told him to do. He didn't really believe her. But as good fortune would have it, he didn't have too long to wait. Soon the entire shoreline was crowded with water bugs swimming and plunging and frolicking. As the water bugs climbed on land, each one transformed into a beautiful woman—each one more attractive, alluring, and beautiful than the next.

"Who are you?" Rabbit Man asked the beautiful creatures emerging from the water.

"We are water bug maidens," they told him. "Our sister sent us for your pleasure."

Rabbit Man thought he had died and gone to heaven. He couldn't believe his eyes. The reveling and pleasuring lasted for four days until Rabbit Man did drop dead and go to heaven. At the end, many of the water bug maidens were pregnant. Those children became the first Water Bug Clan.

Water Bug Clan people are a welcome force of resiliency in these times of failing systems. Listen to the language of water for it whispers the way to this sweet, humble clan. Summon the memory and intelligence of the stream so that it may fill up what is unfulfilled.

WOLF

A wolf's fur color varies from gray to black and it can even be white. Wolves live in packs and the average wolf pack is less than ten. Packs sometimes range over a hundred square miles. Their preferred diet is hoofed animals such as caribou, elk, bison, deer, moose, and others. They can run over thirty-five miles an hour for short distances. Usually they amble along at about five miles per hour.

Wolves have extreme and unbreakable loyalty to one another. They have magical powers and cosmic connections to the moon and all the moon's teachings. Wolf is a guide and the original pathfinder. It is said they know every trail, every footpath, every alleyway, every lane, and every route. They are never lost and they know the way. Wolves have always been known as warriors, hunters, and trackers.

Some members of the Wolf Clan are said to be able to find their way in the dimensions. In the beginning of the world the Great Spirit told the wolves to measure all the land on earth and come back and report what they found. So they did. The wolves know the directions well and the length and breadth of the earth. They have a wide understanding of sacred mathematics and sacred geometry.

The Wolf Clan teaches listening and paying close attention to what is being said or heard. Wolf Clan people are intelligent. They honor and protect their family and their pack. The sound of a pack of wolves breaking out in song and baying into the silence of a moonlit night is spectacular. It sends shivers down your spine and bolsters the human spirit.

Wolves are resilient. They are not egotists who feel they must go it alone. They don't resist help and they know they have a network of sister and brother wolves there for support. The whole pack is concerned about the well-being of each wolf. The pack will comfort, uplift, and aid any individual wolf that needs it.

Members of the Wolf Clan are natural instructors, storytellers, historians, and thinkers. Often, they are the unexpected life of a party. They are cosmically aligned to challenge your principles and make you think. Even in ordinary exchanges, they reveal that you have much to learn.

These people remember they are descended from wolves. They have ceremonies and sing to the moon to honor their ancestors. They are known as protectors of culture, tradition, and the environment. They are also accurate historians. It is said they can see vividly into the past and can make it come alive in front of you. Coyotes and wolves were the first musicians and know the scores. They understand vibration.

Some members of this clan are trained from childhood to learn from nature—the trees, the rocks, and of course the animals. They carry these expanded teachings, along with hundreds of teaching stories, medicine stories, and legends. They have ceremonial knowledge and are known as the greatest of teachers.

Wolf Clan people are called upon during times of turmoil and instability to lead and teach and are an important clan for our present times. To be a part of this clan is to understand how to impart knowledge. Walk through the twilight hours and master your inner and outer territory. The Wolf Clan will show you the way home.

YELLOW FINCH

The yellow finch is one of the loveliest of creatures, a bright golden yellow with black feathers on its wings and twelve yellow tail feathers. It is striking, exquisite. Some say it is a piece of the spiritual sun. Some even say that the yellow finch is an intermediary sent from the sun and carries the medicine power of the spiritual sun. A glance from the bird can be like lightning opening your heart to higher purpose. In flight, the yellow finch is often a study in aerial acrobatics. They dip and dive and it can be a most breathtaking sight. You can see males chasing after the females. In winter they will form into flocks and will forage together for food. Perhaps this is why they are a reminder to eat plenty of protein and have a balanced diet.

Metaphysically, the color yellow conjures up golden rays, joy, powerful intellectual ability, and logical consistency. The yellow finch is the avatar of this color. Step inside the golden medicine circle of the yellow finch and these qualities will abound. This feathered friend reminds you to be optimistic and to let your light shine.

These beautiful birds help farmers immensely. They eat insects and keep weeds down by consuming their seeds. In the fall, males and females usually separate until the spring. As a muse, the yellow finch gives the divine spark that generates creativity and accomplishment. The yellow finch is aware of their inner sun, the spiritual core of their being. This connection gives them a positive, bright disposition.

Members of the Yellow Finch Clan are good-humored and happy. They are always optimistic, a much-needed quality in these current times. They walk into a room and it fills with golden delight. They have joy in their heart because they are connected with sun energy. This connects them cosmically to the harmony of the spheres, which makes them vibrant and unafraid.

Yellow Finch Clan people love life. They are lively and upbeat. Allegiances to this clan are intuitive and spiritual in nature and members of this clan are always incomparable in grace and beauty in their relationships with one another. These people are reminders to be content and joyful, to live the old ways, and to keep life simple and happy—to live drinking in the sunshine.

Yellow Finch Clan members are enthusiastic and will help you begin new projects asking nothing in return. They are natural environmentalists and careful with the earth's resources.

If the sweet trilling of the yellow finch plays inside your head, move to its promise. The Yellow Finch Clan must be near you. Meditate on the inner sun at your solar plexus. The brilliant yellow finch will light the way to golden abundance and happiness in all areas of your life.

YELLOW JACKET

Yellow jackets are common and can be found practically anywhere in the world. The yellow jacket's body is yellow and black striped and has four glassine-like wings. Their faces are yellow with dark eyes. They have large antenna, six legs, and a nasty stinger at the end of their abdomen. They can sting more than once.

Yellow jackets live in colonies and usually eat nectar, pollen, and insects. They build paper nests. Colony inhabitants number in the thousands. Yellow jacket populations are extremely large. Each yellow jacket has a specific job. Workers do the work needed to maintain the nest, the queen lays eggs, and the drones fertilize her when she is ready.

Yellow Jacket Clan people are territorial and have a strong sense of place. They are community minded and work hard for the benefit of everyone. They are social and enjoy large communal groups. Each one of them has a similar collective dream. There is a sort of osmosis of thoughts and concepts between them. They have hivelike rules that may be the most authoritarian in nature but work because they are assimilated by the entire clan. Everyone has marching orders and obeys the hive mother's dictates.

A yellow jacket female has strong life force and exhibits warrior traits such as protecting those she loves. Her loyalties are fierce but she keeps her emotions hidden. She is independent and her social skills are formidable. She is confident, courageous, and well prepared for all contingencies. Don't ever doubt her bravery. Yellow jackets seek a series of small victories. They build. They make. And it adds up to great accomplishment. Their sense of duty never leaves them.

A clan legend tells of a horrible monster that stole yellow jacket children and ran away with them to a concealed hiding place. The yellow jackets searched for them to no avail. The children continued to be taken. The yellow jackets tried to track the monster but were unsuccessful.

The yellow jackets decided to hover high above the children. Then when the monster took the next child, the yellow jackets were ready and followed him in pursuit high, high above. The monster went inside a large cave. As soon as it did, the yellow jackets swarmed inside the entrance and began stinging the monster all at once. The monster writhed and screamed in agony. More yellow jackets swarmed in around him. They didn't relent from stinging the monster until he was dead.

Yellow jackets are aggressive. They swoop down, darting swiftly toward their intended victim or, just as surprisingly, they will fly in low and swoop up for the attack. They are confident strategists. Likewise, the yellow jackets should never be challenged. To do so is folly. Best move on.

On the other hand, if this is your clan, let the yellow jacket energy circulate through you so you can harness it. Trust your deeper knowing. To align with this clan is a step toward personal fulfillment and longevity. Yellow jackets tell you to pull your dreams close so you can stay in touch with them and work toward their completion. The Yellow Jacket Clan has a certain lightness of spirit. Beyond logic, there is the group, the hive, the collective unconscious. Whatever you want to call it, it is the deep wisdom within that leads to your perfect habitation.

6

<del>◄◄◄</del>╫<del>◘</del>╫<del>►►►</del>

THE SPIRIT OF THE
TIME CARRIER

Long ago on the North American continent it was the lowly thirteen-lined chipmunk, or thirteen-lined ground squirrel, that was said to control various aspects of measured time such as time distortions—the movement backward and forward in the time stream. If you met this particular striped chipmunk on your path, there would be some important aspect of time to be reflected upon.

Also known as the spirit of the Time Carrier, the thirteen-lined chipmunk is truly a fantastical being. It carries thirteen lines, which represent the thirteen lunar months of twenty-eight days each and is based on lunar cycles and phases.

If you want to engage with this being, spend some effort familiarizing yourself with its behavior, traits, and presence. Chipmunks are members of the squirrel family. Their bodies are lean and they have puffed cheeks and bushy tails. Their eyes are large and shiny and hurriedly shift their attention in many directions, flitting here and there. They have a disorienting, hypnotic quality. They have a probing curiosity and an exuberance about everything.

This special animal is active at twilight—dusk and dawn, the time when the world changes. They are like bears in that they hibernate and spend long periods of time dreaming. Dreams are a bridge to many alternative laws of time—in dream we no longer experience the linear course of time but instead we can hopscotch to portals holding alternate time realities. We can gaze into the mirror of time, prisms that can change, distort, and reconfigure the quality of time as we know it.

Often an encounter with the thirteen-striped chipmunk caused vivid crossovers into past lives, future lives, or ventures into distant but somehow familiar landscapes—other remembered worlds.

The meditation in the next chapter is dedicated to the spirit of the Time Carrier and for that purpose we ask for the blessing of all chipmunks.

Now we are going to call to the spirit of this animal asking for her ancient blessings and the gift of her amazing powers. Start the process of creative visualization to familiarize yourself with the thirteen-lined chipmunk. Simply make an introduction in your creative imagination. Don't worry about doing anything right or wrong. Let it unfold as it will. Say hello and become acquainted.

To reinforce a connection to the thirteen-lined chipmunk, try some visual stimulus. First, download a public domain picture of a thirteen-lined chipmunk. Alternately, find a picture of this species of chipmunk you like in a library book and check the volume out and take it home with you so you can look at it at your leisure. You might to want to watch some videos of the thirteen-lined chipmunk or other related footage online.

Each night for a few days, weeks, months, hopefully not years, look at the chipmunk's picture before you go to sleep. Ask the chipmunk to signal to you when you both are ready for further adventures. Try to engage your senses and imagine petting, smelling, hearing, and seeing the animal in your mind's eye. Notice all the details you can. Don't try to force anything, however. Just hold the chipmunk in your consciousness and enjoy any interaction and be in the moment. Ask again for the chipmunk's blessing, a blessing from the Time Carrier.

7

THE JOURNEY TO
YOUR ORIGINAL
SPIRIT CLAN

The inner journey to find your first spirit clan can now begin with the help of the thirteen-lined chipmunk. Read over this meditation several times so that you become thoroughly conversant and at ease with it.

- Find a place free of electronics and distractions where you will not be disturbed—somewhere safe and secure. Connect with the spirit of place.

- Have a pen and journal handy in order to write down your experiences when it is time.

- Lie down, get comfortable, and be at peace.

- Take four deep breaths and close your eyes.

- Adjust yourself so that you are perfectly relaxed and contented, letting go of all tension.

- Speak to the thirteen-lined chipmunk spirit. Ask the spirit to be with you and to help you find your original clan.

- Relax and visualize the thirteen-lined chipmunk as large as life standing in front of you. See the lines and the dots between the lines and the curious hypnotic patterns covering her body. The human-sized chipmunk you see is standing in front of a time portal that is filled with blinding white light. Ask the creature to shift time and point the way to your spirit clan. Tell the chipmunk to take you into the portal and bring you to ancient memories. Let the chipmunk take you by the hand and lead you into the exact center of the light and into the portal.

- Once inside, go quickly with the chipmunk to your original clan and ask it to wait for you unobtrusively during your experiences. You will begin to see an image or images of this earliest memory. Look at your feet. What are you wearing? Sit down and be with your clan. Where are you? What are your surroundings like? Are you in a cave? What kind of dwellings does your clan have? Who are you with? Do you see a fire? Do you see food? What kind of food? Are there weapons nearby? If so, what are they? Are the people of your clan dressed in a certain way? Are they wearing ornaments?

- What is your spirit clan? Who is your clan mother? What are your feelings toward her? Are any of the other people greatly familiar to you? What are their beliefs and what is their clan totem? Note everything.

Note each person. Communicate with them, mind to mind. Ask if they will teach you any clan songs, dances, or secrets. Ask for your clan's stories. Ask to be shown any landmarks that are important to your clan. Is there other information your clan wants to share with you? What are your clan's traditions? Try to glean as much information as you can and commit it to conscious recall.

- This may take awhile so go at your own pace. When you are ready, you will want to say goodbye to the people in your clan. Thank them all for being there in memory. Tell them you are happy to find them and that you will be back to visit and to learn more from them. Say goodbye and tell the thirteen-lined chipmunk to take you back though the time portal. Once through, thank the chipmunk for helping you. Say goodbye to the chipmunk and tell her you will continue to seek her help.

- And now, slowly returning in your own way to full waking consciousness in the present, open your eyes.

- Awake and happy for your experience and remembering all, write in your journal.

Note that this is the work. It can be a deep emotional cleansing, this reconnection with the primal energy of your original spirit clan. It has the possibility of revivifying your life force and blessing you in certain new ways. Once you see your passages through previous lives clearly, that in itself is a great cleansing and release, a worthy reward for your effort—releasing you from suffering and birthing you to a new freedom.

This work is presented as an art form, a forgotten language, a springboard into self-exploration and discovery. Spirit clans are a story, a tale, our earliest of zeitgeists.

Once upon a lost and distant time, spirit clans were the lens through which our ancestors interpreted the world. The discovery of your spirit clan is like waking up from amnesia and remembering when people communicated from their heart.

8

OF TIME AND TIME TRAVEL

Perhaps by now you have had an epiphany or at least a glimpse of your spirit clan. If you are at the beginning of your journey into past lives, you will want to keep the path in front of you swept clean of confusion, lack of focus, laziness, or any other impediment. It is a special kind of encounter you are seeking in order to set yourself free from the bindings of past lives that are holding you back in your present life. Seeking within yourself a knowledge of all previous incarnations and an awakening of your lost identity—your spiritual heritage—that is the work.

This shamanic work is a compass that points the way to triumph over ignorance and confusion. Embrace the possibility and light. May you be reunited with your spirit clan, come to know your true self as prophets and philosophers have always taught, and know that what you seek, you will find.

ABOUT THE AUTHOR

DAVID CARSON is a writer living in Taos, New Mexico. Born and raised in Oklahoma, he spent extensive time with Native American elders, clan mothers, knowledge keepers, story-tellers, healers, shamans, and "holy" men and women. He is the coauthor of the bestselling *Medicine Cards: The Discovery of Power Through the Ways of Animals.*

HAMPTON ROADS
PUBLISHING COMPANY

... for the evolving human spirit

Hampton Roads Publishing Company publishes books on a variety of subjects, including spirituality, health, and other related topics.

For a copy of our latest trade catalog, call (978) 465-0504 or visit our distributor's website at *www.redwheelweiser.com*. You can also sign up for our newsletter and special offers by going to *www.redwheelweiser.com/newsletter/*.